User's Manual

BUSINESS PLAN

Visit our career web site at:
www.careercity.com

Our corporate web site:
www.adamsmedia.com

And coming soon our business web site at:
www.businesstown.com

TABLE OF CONTENTS

This page intentionally blank.

INTRODUCTION & INSTALLATION INSTRUCTIONS

Welcome to Adams Streetwise Complete Business Plan

About the Program:

Adams Streetwise Complete Business Plan was designed to serve as a comprehensive multimedia guide to creating a complete business plan to raise money - or to run your small business.

Designed for the real world, Adams Streetwise Complete Business Plan addresses the tough issues head-on. The issues that bankers and investors really care about; the issues that will determine your success in the real world. Your plan needs to include: A realistic competitive analysis. A strategy that sets you apart form the competition. A marketing plan that fits your budget. Sales and profitability projections that you can justify and achieve! That's the kind of plan you'll create with Adams Streetwise Complete Business Plan.

Whether you're starting a one-person business or managing an established enterprise, a good business plan can really help you succeed! Here are the Five major parts of this program:

Business Plan Text

Summary. The foundation for the rest of the plan including your business concept, your current situation, your key success factors, and your financial needs.

Vision. The future vision that you have for your company. Plus more specific goals, such as sales and profit targets.

Market. A careful analysis of the market including marketplace trends, market segments, customer needs, customer characteristics, and busying habits.

Competitors. Compare differences, strengths, and weaknesses of competing products or services, and competing companies.

Strategy. By identifying your key competitive capabilities and the opportunities in the marketplace, you'll be able to choose a strategy that is right for you business.

Products. Position your products or services successfully against the competition by using your competitive analysis.

Marketing. Develop marketing, sales, and advertising plans that support your company strategy and send a consistent message.

Operations. From evaluating key personnel to the adequacy of your current facilities, this is an important part of every plan.

Misc. Items you'll need to put the finishing touches on your plan. Includes: Cover letter, non-disclosure statement, title page and table of contents.

Business Plan Financial

Assumptions & Comments. The basic information about your business. This will include whether you purchase inventory or sell on credit, pay commissions and other basic information.

Starting Balance Sheet. This is the information on where your business is today.

Profit and Loss Projection. Plug in your numbers to get a picture of where your business should be at the end of the duration of your plan.

Cash Flow Projection. This will determine financing requirements of your business.

Balance Sheet Projection. The Balance Sheet fills in as a result of the information that you have already provided in the Assumptions, Starting Balance Sheet, Profit and Loss Projection and Cash Flow Projection.

Key Ratios and Analysis. This is automatically created for you based on previous entries. You will get a snapshot of your business based on assets to liabilities, profitability to sales, sales break even and more.

Workshops

Numerous multi-media or text based workshops help you get started creating your business plan and task related business issues.

Sample Plans

Sample plans are provided to give you a hint at what you plan should look like.

Question and Answers

Answers to questions you are likely to ask about creating a business plan, getting finfcing adn starting a business

Product Support:

Before you can receive technical support, you must fill out and mail or fax your product registration card to Adams Media Corporation. Your registration information must be on file in order to assist you with Adams Streetwise Complete Business Plan and to notify you of product upgrades and special offers. If you have not already registered Adams Streetwise Complete Business Plan, you may do so with your first support call.

How to Reach Us:

By Mail: Adams Media Corporation
260 Center Street
Holbrook, MA 02343

By phone: (781) 767-4128

By Fax: (781) 767-2055

By email: support@adamsmedia.com

Before Calling Technical Support:

We understand that there might be times when you will encounter some problems in running Adams Streetwise Complete Business Plan. Before contacting us, take a few minutes to review the following to see if you can alleviate the problem yourself.

1. Make sure your system complies with the requirements outlined in the Getting Started section.

2. Make sure your computer functions properly without Adams Streetwise Complete Business Plan installed on your hard drive.

If these steps do not provide you with a satisfactory solution, contact Adams Media Technical Support.

Calling Technical Support:

Technical Support hours are Monday through Friday, between 9 AM and 5 PM, Eastern Time. Before calling, please make sure your computer is turned on, with Adams Streetwise Complete Business Plan running and on the screen. When you reach an Adams Media technical support specialist, be prepared to give the following information:

◆ The version of Adams Streetwise Complete Business Plan (Located in the Options>About section of the program)

◆ The type of computer you are using (486, Pentium, model, etc.)

◆ The operating system software you are using (Windows 3.1, Windows for Workgroups 3.11, Windows 95/98, Windows NT)

Email Support:

You can contact us any time, day or night the Internet. We are usually able to respond within 24 hours.

Getting Started:

The following are the system requirements for using Adams Streetwise Complete Business Plan.

Windows System Requirements:

◆ 486 PC compatible or higher
◆ 5 MB of free hard disk space
◆ 4 MB of RAM (8 MB recommended)
◆ 256 color VGA graphics card, (SVGA recommended)
◆ Sound Blaster or compatible audio card (not required for lite version)

◆ Windows95 or higher, Windows 3.1x or Windows NT
◆ Mouse
◆ 2X or better CD-ROM drive, for multimedia version

Installing Adams Streetwise Complete Business Plan:

There are two options for installing Adams Streetwise Complete Business Plan on Windows computers. One method is used if you are running Windows 95 or higher or Windows NT 4.0, and the other method is used if you are running Windows for Workgroups 3.11 , Windows 3.1 or Windows NT 3.51.

Special Note to Users of Lotus 1-2-3 version 5 before Lotus 97: We feel you can do all the work you need to develop top notch financials with our Complete Business Plan. However, the spreadsheets you develop within our program can be exported to Lotus 97 and Microsoft Excel for further modification. You cannot export the spreadsheets you develop within our program into any version of Lotus 1-2-3 prior to Lotus 97.

If, after familiarizing yourself with our spreadsheets, you decide you would like to use a version of Lotus which is not compatible with our program to develop your financials, you can do so based on our setup. We have provided a fully functional Lotus 5 version of the spreadsheets you can use to do so. All the formulas, calculations and as much of the functionality as these early versions of Lotus allowed is included in these spreadsheets. The file is called LOT_FIN and can be found in the Lotus directory on the CD-ROM. To open these spreadsheets, follow these steps:

1. Start Lotus 1-2-3 and choose File, then Open.
2. Change drives so that you are looking at the root directory of the CD-ROM.
3. Double-click on the directory named Lotus.
4. You should see the Lotus File LOT_FIN. Double-click on it to open it.

Windows 95, Windows 98, and Windows NT 4.0

1. Insert the Adams Streetwise Complete Business Plan CD into your CD-ROM drive.
2. The installation routine will begin automatically. If the installation does not begin, then choose Run from the taskbar and type "D:SETUP". If you are using another CD-ROM drive letter, substitute it for D:.
3. Confirm or change the installation subdirectory.

Windows for Workgroups 3.11, Windows 3.1, or Windows NT 3.51

1. Insert the Adams Streetwise Complete Business Plan CD into your CD-ROM drive.
2. From the Windows Program Manager, choose Run from the File menu.
3. Type D:SETUP in the Run dialog box. If you are using another CD-ROM drive address, substitute its drive letter for D:.
4. The installation routine will begin.
5. Confirm or change the installation subdirectory.

Please note: The CD-ROM version of this product will only work if the CD is in your CD-ROM drive while you are running the program.

This page intentionally blank.

QUICK START—CREATING YOUR BUSINESS PLAN

For those of you who are business plan and computer savvy, require minimal information, and hate reading users manuals.

1) Click on the Business Plan icon in the Main Menu [See Screen Shot 1]. Select the appropriate option from the Business Plan Text dialog box and you will get to the Text screen.

2) Choose the section and subsection you wish to work on from the Menu Bar at the top of the page. Scroll through the choices in the upper box until you find the one that best suits your needs. Double click on the chosen paragraph.

3) Once you have selected a paragraph it will appear in the lower half of your screen where you may edit it and fill in missing information. Repeat this step for each section of the business plan you are interested in including. Save the plan using the ".pln" extension.

4) Print the text portion of the business plan.

5) After you have finished with the text section of your business plan return to the Main Menu and again click on the Business Plan icon. Select Business Plan Financials in the dialog box and you will get to the Financials Screen.

6) It is important that you input the data for the financials in order as much of the data is linked throughout the financial reports. Begin with Assumptions and Comments, second enter data on Starting Balance Sheet and the third step is the Profit and Loss Forecast. Cash Flow and Balance Sheet Projections will require minimal data entry one the first three components are completed.

7) Print the financial part of the business plan.

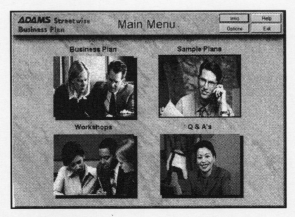

Screen Shot 1

This page intentionally blank.

BUSINESS PLAN TEXT—THE BASICS

The Business Plan text portion of the program is designed to allow you to develop a thorough description of your business, your market, and your overall strategy with a minimum effort. You can also export the text to any word processor for further revision.

Once you are in the Business Plan Text part of the program, you can choose any of the topics listed in the lower menu bar - Summary, Vision, Market etc. Each choice will give you a menu of sections you can include in your Business Plan.

For instance, under Summary, you can choose Business Concept. Some key questions, along with a selection of various paragraphs you can include in your Business Plan for various situations, will appear in the upper half of the Word Processor. After reading each selection, double-click on the paragraph you think will be most useful to you. It will appear in the lower half of the screen where you can edit to fit your situation.

If you want to enter a second paragraph, double-click on it. If your cursor is located within a previously written paragraph when you click on it, you will be asked to choose whether to append the text to the bottom of the current listing or insert it in the middle. Make the appropriate selection and choose OK. Note that if you check off "Don't Ask me Again" in this Dialog Box, this question will not re-appear unless you go to the View Menu and check off Paste Options.

To use standard Windows Cut, Copy, and Paste functions (in Windows 95), right click anywhere on the screen with your mouse and use the commands as you would in any word processor. To use these commands in Windows 3.1x, consult the following list:

Cut   -   CTRL X
Copy -   CTRL C
Paste -   CTRL V
Undo -   CTRL Z

If none of the paragraphs are appropriate, you can create your own by typing in the lower half of the box.

After you are through with the text of the one section of the Business Plan, go to the Summary, Vision, Marketing menu items and choose another one to work on. Note that most business plan writers will choose not to include all of the sections listed. In fact, some writers may wish to only include a few of the most important sections. This many options are merely offered to you as a guide for preparing your plan.

After you have completed the text of your plan, you can view it by choosing Print Preview. This will show all the sections of your plan. You can move from page to page by hitting Next and Previous. To move to the End of a Plan hit Bottom, to the beginning hit Top in the Print Preview Window. Back will return you to the Business Plan Text Selection Screen.

To save the plan, choose save in the file menu. The Save dialogs work as standard Windows functions. You can also use the Quick Save button to do a save while you are working.

There are a number of additional functions in the view menu. Choosing Full Screen view in this menu, will bring the particular section of the Business Plan you are working in into full screen view, hiding the pre-formatted paragraph window in the program. To return to viewing the pre-formatted paragraphs we have given you in half screen view, choose Split Screen.

The Paste Options turns off and On the dialog box regarding the inserting of a paragraph at the end of the text or in the middle as described above.

The Large, Medium, and Small Font views in this menu change the viewing of the text for ease of readability. Note that they change this for the entire window - they are not formatting functions.

Opening a Previous File

You can open a previous file from either the File menu in the Word Processing part of the program or in the original opening dialog box when prompted to choose between Loading a previous Business Plan or Start a new one.

If, in one session with our program, you do the following:

1) Open a Business Plan Text, make some changes to it, save it, then quit out of the Business Plan Text part of the Program.
2) Return to the Business Plan Text of the program.

You will automatically be taken into the Business Plan you were working on most recently. This is a feature of the program to make it easier for you to continue your work when switching back and forth between financials and text. If you want to open a different file or start a new one at this point, choose File, then New or File, then Open as is appropriate for your situation.

Export Instructions

While we do not think that you need to fancy up a business plan document provided it is well written and concise, we do realize that some users will want to export these Business Plan files for further revision in their word processors. You can export these documents easily to any Word Processor. To do so, follow these instructions.

1) In the Business Plan Text File Menu, choose Export. (Note that this function will not be available till you have done a Save).
2) If you have not done a recent save of the current text of the document, you will be prompted to do so. It is very important to note that the export function only exports what is saved, not what is one the screen. So if you are prompted to save the document before the export can take place, do it.
3) The Export Window will appear. This window functions just like a standard Windows save dialog box. Choose the appropriate directory and choose save. The program will save your file as a text document.

To open this program from a word processor, follow these steps. (Please note that some word processors have slightly different interfaces than the one described. If you are confused about how to open these documents in your specific word processor, check in your word processor's help files for information on how to open text documents. If you still have problems, contact our technical support department - please have the name and version number of the word processing program ready when you call)

1) Start your word processor. Under the file Menu, choose Open.

2) Move to the directory where you saved your Business Plan. Then change the Files of Type choice in the Open Dialog Box to Text Documents (.txt). You should see your document in the file window if your are in the right directory. Double-click on it and it should open. If your word processor prompts you as to what file format to convert the file from, choose Text.

3) You should be able to make whatever changes you want to the file at this point. When you are done save the file in the word processors proprietary format to insure your changes are kept.

Things You Should Know

Please be aware of the following when you are using our program.

1) If you do not have a printer installed, the Print Preview Window will come up blank. Because this is the only way to view your entire plan, you may want to install a printer driver off the Windows install disks to bring the plan into view. For information on how to do this, see your Windows documentation. If you still have problems, please contact our technical support.

2) If you double-click on a file after an export, it will open in Notepad on most computers. This is a standard Windows setting - and one you should probably not change. Follow the instructions above for opening an exported file and you should not have any problems.

3) Double-clicking on a file with the .pln extension (a non-exported Business plan file) will not open it in our program even if you were to associate this extension with our program in your Windows settings. Do not do this - you may cause system problems. To open a Business Plan file, start the Business Plan program, go into the Business Plan Text part of our program and either choose to open it from the Dialog Box, which allows you to choose whether to open a previous Business Plan or Start a new one, or from the File menu in the actual word processing part of our program.

4) Exporting is a one way process. You cannot open an exported file from our program, though you can open up its corresponding Business Plan (.pln) version for further editing from within our program.

This page intentionally blank.

BUSINESS PLAN FINANCIALS—THE BASICS

About the financials

These financial statements offer a very fast and efficient way to create complete integrated financial statements for any business. They also allow you to change a single assumption and instantly see how these changes will impact every financial statement.

Level of detail of financial statements

These financials show an appropriate amount of detail for preparing a business plan. They intentionally do not show the minute detail that may be appropriate for individual department budgets used in a medium or larger business. Financiers, be they equity investors or bank lenders do not want to see the minute details of your budgets. Similarly if you are preparing a business plan to help run your business better, you need to first focus on a plan that does not have too many levels of detail. Otherwise you will get caught up in the detail and lose sight and control of the overall direction of the business.

Choice of financial statements

For all but the smallest businesses the financial statements that you should prepare are highly standard: profit and loss projection, cash flow projection and balance sheet projection. However for some very small businesses that are not seeking outside financing and do not expect any cash flow shortfalls you may choose to only prepare a profit and loss projection.

Format of financial statements

While the choice of financial statements is highly standard, the form of each financial statement varies somewhat depending on who is preparing it, although all financial statements contain certain required elements. If you have ever prepared financial statements before, chances are that you used a format somewhat different than those included in this package. Don't worry--everyone includes different items or levels of detail in their financials. Bankers and investors are used to seeing financials in many different formats.

By using the financials in this software you will be able to very quickly create integrated financials and instantly change assumptions. These benefits will outweigh any initial discomfort you may have in using financials that may be formatted a little differently than financials you have used in the past. Note also that at the bottom of the Assumptions page you can customize many of the profit and loss headings.

You can export the financials at any stage to your own spreadsheet program to customize them any way you choose. However, we recommend that you work in the program as much as possible and avoid the extra work in exporting the financials. Keep in mind that bankers and potential equity investors see a large variety of formats of financial statements. A note to Lotus 1-2-3 users: As this program will only export in Microsoft Excel format (.xls) you will need to choose .xls as a file type when opening the file in Lotus.

Moving from one spreadsheet to the next

You can use the tabs at the top of the spreadsheets to move from one financial spreadsheet to the next. Moving from one spreadsheet to another will not affect data.

Sequence to Work on Spreadsheets

It is strongly recommended that you work on the financial spreadsheets in the following order:

1. Assumptions and Comments
2. Starting Balance Sheet
3. Profit and Loss Projection
4. Cash Flow Projection
5. Balance Sheet Projection
6. Key Ratios and Analysis

This is important because information generally flows between the spreadsheets according to order listed above.

Automatic copying function

Because we know that many users want to create financial spreadsheets very quickly with as little work as possible, many appropriate rows on the spreadsheets have an automatic copying function, that automatically copies your entry from one cell to the subsequent cells in the following months. Similarly, in these same rows, entries that you make in these cells will total to the current year and then be anualized for future years of your plan. If you don't want the same entry in following months or years, you can simply overwrite the entries.

Overwriting formulas on spreadsheets

Generally, on the spreadsheets you can overwrite formulas that may change for some businesses. However, formulas that will always be appropriate such as adding up or subtracting items in a category may not be changed. We suggest however, that you avoid overwriting formulas as much as possible and let the software do the work for you. Remember, you can instantly create a new financial scenario by changing any answer on the Assumptions spreadsheet.

If you elect to overwrite a formula you must use the Microsoft Excel format which is to start the formula with an equal (=) sign. Failure to do this will result in an error message. Note that if for any reason you change you mind and wish to use the original formula that was provided you may do so by pressing the "Esc" (escape) key. Also note, however, that once you have hit the enter key you can not restore the original formula.

About the colors of the numbers

As you look at the spreadsheets on your computer screen, you will notice that the numbers are in different colors. This is to help you use the spreadsheets--the numbers and rest of the information on the spreadsheets will print in black color, to make your financial statements appear as professional as possible. This is what the colors mean:

Green: You should enter data into these cells. You will not overwrite any formulas.

Red: You can not enter data into these cells, they are locked. They are determined by formula.

Purple: You can enter data into these cells, but you will overwrite formulas. Anytime you make an entry into one of these cells, you will overwrite and lose the formula in the cell. Some of the cells that have purple numbers have formulas that interact with other spreadsheets. Other cells that have purple numbers have formulas that merely help you to enter numbers more quickly, by copying the entry that you made into the first month or year, into subsequent months or years.

Creating your own formulas for spreadsheets

The spreadsheets are set up so that you don't have to create any formulas yourself. All you need to do is enter your own data. However, you can create your own formulas to speed entering data or to replace the existing formulas. The formulas need to follow the Excel spreadsheet format, regardless of what spreadsheet program you personally use on your computer. The Excel format is: "=(operation)". For example, to have cell C5 have 50% of the value of cell B5, you would enter in cell C5: "=(.50*B5).

Note that the cell number is displayed in the upper left corner of the spreadsheet window [see Screen Shot 2].

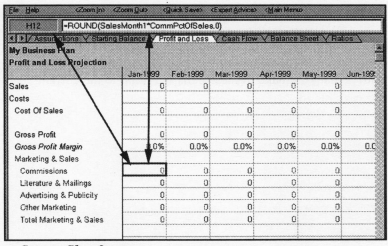

Screen Shot 2

Number format and rounding of numbers

The numbers are intended to be presented in whole dollars. Results of formulas are automatically truncated to the nearest dollar. There are a few exceptions such as ratio's that are rounded to either one or two decimal places.

Rounding "Errors"

Because results of formulas are rounded to the nearest dollar, there may appear to be slight rounding "errors" if you compare the results of these financials to another method. Rounding "errors" may compound slightly when results are added from one column to the next. For example a five dollar rounding "error" may occur when comparing the 12th month of a balance sheet prepared using rounding with one prepared not using rounding.

You should not at all be concerned about such rounding "errors" and they should not be even thought of as errors at all. This is a business plan, not a physics equation. Potential bankers or equity lenders will not be concerned about minor rounding issues. If you want you can note that "Some numbers may not be exact to the last digit due to rounding in formulas." We suggest that you do not over-ride numbers to try to correct rounding issues particularly because you may need to overwrite formulas, and your financial statements will really not be any better.

Working in thousands

If you are planning a larger business, you could enter all amounts on the spreadsheets in thousands (000's). For example instead of entering projected first month sales of "151,343" you could just enter "151." Using thousands will make your spreadsheets less crowded and easier to read. For smaller businesses however, rounding entries to the nearest thousands will significantly change the meaning of your financial statements and should not be done. Please note that working in thousands will compound dramatically any "rounding errors" that occur.

Saving spreadsheets

To save spreadsheets click on File, then to save for the first time click on Save-as. Then choose a name for your spreadsheets. To save additional times you can simply click on Save.

Because the spreadsheets interact with one another data is saved from the spreadsheets as a set. In other words every time you save spreadsheet data you will save data for the Assumptions, the Starting Balance Sheet, the Profit and Loss Projection, the Cash Flow Projection, the Balance Sheet Projection and the Ratios. It is not possible to save just one of these spreadsheets [*See Screen Shot 3*]. You will also need to complete work on the individual cell you are entering data to before saving. All menu items are disabled for your protection when a cell is active.

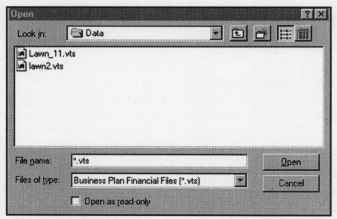

Screen Shot 3

Printing spreadsheets

In printing you can either choose to print the spreadsheet you are working on or the entire workbook. Select File from the Menu bar, click on print, then click OK in the print dialog box. Note that these spreadsheets contain a huge amount of information in comparison to most items that you print. Printing an entire workbook may simply overwhelm your printer.

To troubleshoot this problem, print out the spreadsheets individually. Be patient when doing this - even printing a single spreadsheet may take a while.

If this does not work, try following these steps (Windows 95 only).

1) Go to your My Computer icon and double-click.
2) Double-click on the Printer icon
3) Highlight the printer you are using and go under the File menu and choose Properties.
4) Click on the Details Tab.
5) Hit the button for Spool Settings
6) Write down you current setting for spool data format.
7) Check off Print directly to Printer.
8) Close all the dialog boxes you have opened and re-start our program.

If you try printing now, it should work, though it may be slow. If this does not work, please contact technical support.

To restore your former printer settings, follow the steps above, but choose Spool printer jobs so printing finishes faster and restore your spool data format to what you wrote down above.

Spreadsheet printing format

Inside the program each spreadsheet is designed to print on one page of standard 8 1/2 x 11 paper in landscape style (Assumptions and Ratios print on one page 8 1/2 x 11 portrait). Having each spreadsheet on just one page makes them much easier to review and analyze. If you want to use a different printing format you will have to export the data to your spreadsheet program.

30 day months, 360 day years

For the purpose of even division and continuity your financials will be prepared using a "Standard Bank Year" method. That means that each month is figured to have 30 days and the year will total 360 days.

Getting familiar with financials

Especially if you have little experience creating financials, we suggest that you first get familiar with how these financials interact by creating a very simple test scenario--such as a business with no sales on credit, no inventory, no payables and only one or two expense categories. Then observe how the Assumptions, the Starting Balance Sheet, the Profit and Loss Projection, the Cash Flow Projection, the Balance Sheet Projection and the Ratios interact with one another.

Tracing problems/issues with your financials

In working with financial statements it is easy to become overwhelmed by the huge amount of data and the numerous worksheets. So the first rule of thumb is to not panic, and to simplify your focus. For example if every month of your balance sheet is wrong, begin by focusing exclusively on the first month. Focus on one item at a time to try to determine where the problem is originating. For data that is determined by other financial spreadsheets or by the Assumptions, trace your problem back to where the data originated from, and be sure that you have input the correct data.

Should you export your financial spreadsheets?

We suggest that as much as possible you work on the financials inside the program, and only export them if you feel that you need to make a significant change that can not be made inside the program. This program has been designed to make it as easy as possible to work on financial spreadsheets, and you will probably find it more difficult to work on them outside of the program. Also worth noting is that while you can export to Excel or 1-2-3 you may not import. This means that you will not be able to bring back any work you have done on a program outside Complete Business Plan.

Some users may feel an urge to "dress up" their financials for presentation purposes, but we would advise against this. Bankers and equity investors aren't going to be impressed by fancy typefaces or colors in your financial statements. If you wish to have greater detail in your financials you can export this plan to Microsoft Excel or Lotus 1-2-3. A note of caution here, unless you are familiar with these spreadsheets and are comfortable writing formulas you will be best served by using the forms we have provided.

Exporting financials to Excel

To export financials to your own spread sheet click on the file menu and select Export. Give your spreadsheets a File Name and make sure that the "*.xls" file format is chosen. Then start Excel and open the file. Files exported out of Complete Business Plan can be read by Excel 5.0 and higher. Exported spreadsheets are write protected and you will need to disable this prior to working on the spreadsheet

Exporting financials to Lotus 1-2-3 '97

To export financials to your own spread sheet click on the file menu and select Export. Give your spreadsheets a File Name and choose the "*.xls" file format, this will be your only option in Save As. Then start Lotus and open the file, and select the Excel (*.xls;*.xlt;*.xlw) file type from the File Type box in the open file screen. At this time you can save the file with a Lotus extension (.wk*).

Exporting for users of earlier versions of Lotus 1-2-3

For users of previous versions of Lotus 1-2-3 we are including a file in the data folder for your use (check readme file for exact file name and location). Also note that if you are planning to use this instead of the internal spreadsheets you should do all of your financials in Lotus as any work done with Complete Business Plan will note be transferred to this file.

ASSUMPTIONS AND COMMENTS

How Assumptions Interact with the other financial spreadsheets

Your answers to the Assumptions will affect results for all relevant numbers in the other financial statements. For example if you reduce your payroll tax rate, you will reduce your expenses on your Profit and Loss Projection, reduce your use of funds on your Cash Flow Projection and increase the equity on your Balance Sheet Projection. However, changes you input on the financial spreadsheets will not change the answers to the set-up questions.

Answers to Assumptions can be changed at anytime

At anytime while using these financial spreadsheets you can return to Assumptions and change your response to any question. This will automatically recalculate any relevant part of the financial spreadsheets. For example, if after completing all of the financial statements you go back to Assumptions and change the average collection period from 45 to 30 days, then the Cash Flow Projection and the Balance Sheet Projection will both reflect more cash on hand.

Default Answers

Each assumption starts with a default answer to show you exactly where and how to enter your response. Over-write any or all default answers to suit your needs. [*See Screen Shot 4*].

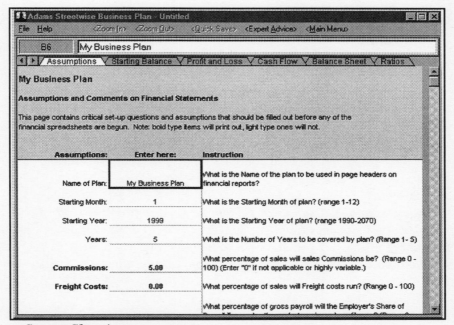

Screen Shot 4

Filling In The Assumptions

Name of Plan

What is the Name of the plan to be used in page headers on financial reports?

If this is the final copy of your plan for presentation you may want to enter the name of your business on it or you may choose to leave it blank. If you are still working on your rough drafts of your financials this line allows you to clearly label each draft, i.e. draft1, draft2, etc.

Starting Month

What is the Starting Month of the plan? (e.g. 1=January)

Enter the starting month of the plan. This, in most instances, should reflect the beginning of your fiscal year.

Starting Year

What is the Starting Year of the plan? (e.g. 1999)

Enter the starting year of the plan. Be sure to enter the full four digits of the year. This has been programmed this way to avoid year 2000 issues.

What is the Number of Years to be covered by plan (Range 1-5)

You can choose to run your plan for 1, 2, 3, 4 or 5 years. Most people create business plans for either one, two or three years. In this fast changing world projections more than 12 months in the future have increasingly little accuracy. The business plan financials are broken out by month for the first year, total for the first year; and then by totals for subsequent years.

Commissions

What percentage of sales will sales Commissions be?

Enter 0 if not applicable or highly variable. (Range 0-100).

If your business pays sales commissions enter the average amount here. For example if you pay 5% commission enter "5", not ".05" or "5%." Entering a "%" will generate an error message. If you do not pay commissions, enter 0. If your business uses dedicated sales staff or pays out finders fees, what percentage does it represent? If you're not sure divide the total commission paid by your sales for the past year.

Freight costs

What percentage of sales will Freight costs run? (Range 0-100)

If your business pays freight or delivery costs enter the average amount here, as a percentage of sales. If you do not have freight costs, enter 0. If you figure freight costs into your cost of goods sold it will be accounted for in inventory value - do not enter it here.

Payroll tax rate

What percentage of gross payroll will the Employer's Share of Payroll Taxes plus the cost of employee benefits run? (Range 0 to 100)

Here you should estimate all of the employer's share of payroll taxes that you will pay plus any fringe benefits such as health care costs, life insurance, etc. Payroll taxes vary with a lot of different factors such as your firm's unemployment rating, the level of pay of each employee and so many other factors that trying to get an exact estimate can be a tedious chore. So you may want to take a rough estimate of the employer's share of payroll taxes, say 13%, and add on an additional percentage for fringe benefits.

Income tax rate

What percentage of net income do you estimate all Income Taxes (city, state, federal) will run? (Range 0-100)

A quick way to roughly estimate your tax rate is to take your estimated federal and state tax rate (and local if applicable) and add them together. (i.e. 30% estimated federal tax rate plus 10% estimated state tax rate adds up to a 40% total tax rate.) Note, if you want to be more precise you could take into consideration that currently in the US the state income tax is deductible from the federal income tax.

Days Inventory

How many Days of Inventory (in other words how many days of sales it would take to exhaust the inventory if it were not replenished) you will stock? (Range 0 to 1080). (If your business will not have inventory enter 0.)

This program is set up to automatically forecast buying inventory when you are short of the Days of Inventory on hand that you enter here. The computer program will evaluate your desired days on hand versus the sales for the current month. For example if you sell 23 apples in January and you enter 30 Days of Inventory the computer will forecast that you buy enough apples to end the month of January with exactly 23 apples on hand for future sales. If you sell 40 apples in February the computer will forecast that you buy enough apples to end the month of February with exactly 40 apples on hand for future sales.

Remember that for this software we are assuming 30 days in each month and 360 days in each year.

Projecting inventory is a very complicated aspect of forecasting. If you can use this software's method of inventory planning you will tremendously simplify your business planning process. Remember that after you are done with your business plan you can come back and instantly create another business plan by inputting another assumption for inventory.

If you believe your amount of inventory on hand will vary between 30 and 60 days inventory on hand, we suggest you follow one of two alternatives. Our first recommendation would be to simply use the average amount of 45 for your Days of Inventory. In your assumptions accompanying your business plan you can state your inventory assumption. Or you could create three scenarios, varying the Days of Inventory from 30 to 45 to 60.

Having inventory will significantly complicate your business planning process. So for example if you are running a house painting service and you buy paint more or less for each job but do not stockpile large quantities of paint, I would recommend that you do not consider the paint to be inventory--but instead an expense item. In other words as soon as you buy the paint I would consider it expensed and I would not consider it to be inventory on hand. (On your tax returns however you technically should include unused paint as an asset.)

Cost of Sales

What percentage of sales will cost of sales (inventory) be? (Range 0-100). Enter 0 if you will not have cost of sales.

Cost of sales are your direct costs of the materials or services that you have sold. For a manufacturing business you would include the costs of the product you are making. You will want to include all expenses that are related such as salaries of manufacturing personnel, raw materials, etc. For a retailer or wholesaler cost of sales is the cost you incurred for products that you have sold not the cost of products still remaining in inventory.

For a service business cost of sales is your direct expenses of providing your service which would typically consist largely of labor costs--that is the labor costs of the people who are directly providing the service, not the support staff. For a restaurant, cost of sales is the cost of the food and beverages that you purchase.

Cost of Sales does not include costs that are not directly incorporated in a finished product or service. For example: marketing costs such as advertising, literature and sales commissions, are not considered costs of sales. General and Administrative expenses, building rent, utilities, and insurance are also not costs of sales.

For costs that you include under costs of sales be sure not to include them in any other categories such as payroll.

Credit Sales? Y/N

Enter Y if you will make Sales on Credit, enter N if you will not.

Even if only a small percentage of your sales will be on credit you should enter "Y", otherwise enter "N." Unless every time you make a sale or provide a service you receive cash or a check you are issuing credit, even if you receive your money in a matter of days. Note if you answer no then you must enter 0 for Accounts Receivable on the Starting Balance Sheet as monies will never be collected

Also note if you enter no here your answer to Credit Sale % and Days Credit will have no effect on spread sheet totals. If you make changes to run different scenarios at a later time then make certain to adjust all of the effected sections

If you take credit cards I would suggest that you consider credit card sales to be cash sales especially if you are reimbursed by the bank for these sales the same day or the next day or two. (Credit card fees may be either handled as an expense item on your Profit and Loss Projection or you can reduce your sales projection to reflect net sales revenue after deducting credit card fees.)

Credit Sales %

Enter % of your sales that will be made on credit. (Range 0-100). Enter 0 if you will not make sales on credit.

Most non-retail businesses will be at or near 100% credit for this question. Retail businesses may be near 100% cash.

Days Credit

How many days will credit customers take on average to pay you (Range 0 - 90). Enter 0 if you will not make sales on credit.

Enter the average number of days that credit customers will pay you. Don't include in the average the fact that cash customers will pay you instantly, because your cash sales payments will be calculated separately.

Remember this software considers all months to have 30 days. So if you expect customers to pay you in one month you should enter "30."

If you believe your average amount of days it takes credit customers to pay will vary, such as between 30 and 60 days, we suggest you follow one of two alternatives. Our first recommendation would be to simply use the average amount of 45 for your days credit assumption. Or you could create three scenarios, varying the days of credit assumption from 30 to 45 to 60.

Cost of Sales A/P Y/N

Will you pay for cost of sales expenses on credit? Enter Y if yes, N if no. A/P is short for accounts payable.

For this answer focus only on credit for Cost of Sales expenses, not marketing or general administrative expenses. If you pay for any costs of sales expenses on credit you should answer "Y" here. Otherwise answer "N." Note, if you answer no to this question then entries for Cost of Sales A/P % and Days Cost of Sales A/P will have no effect on spreadsheet totals.

Cost of Sales A/P %

What percentage of Cost of Sales expenses will be paid for on credit. (Range 0-100.)

For example if you buy 25% of your inventory or other cost of sales expenses on credit then enter "25".

Days Cost of Sales A/P

How many days will you take to pay for Cost of Sales expenses? (Range 0 - 90)

Enter the average number of days that you will pay for inventory or other Cost of Sales expenses that you buy on credit. Don't include in the average any items that you pay for in cash because cash purchases will be calculated separately.

If you believe the average amount of days it takes you to pay for inventory or Cost of Sales expenses varies, such as from 30 to 60 days we suggest one of the two alternatives. Our first recommendation would be to simply use the average amount of 45 for your days. In your assumptions accompanying your business plan you can state this assumption. Or you could create three scenarios, varying the days you take to pay for direct cost items from 30 to 45 to 60.

General A/P Y/N

Other than Cost of Sales expenses will you buy other expense items on credit? Enter "Y" for yes. "N" for no.

This item includes most non inventory and non cost of sales expenses. It includes most marketing and general and administrative costs, but it does not include payroll costs and non-operating costs and depreciation and income taxes. If you buy any non inventory or non cost of sales items on credit you should answer "Y" here. Otherwise answer 'N" for no. Note, if you answer no to this question then entries for General A/P % and Days General A/P will have no effect on spreadsheet totals.

General A/P %

What percentage of non cost of sales (or non-inventory) items or services will be bought on credit? (Range 0-100). Enter 0 if you will not buy these items on credit.

For example if you buy 75% of non payroll-related and non cost of sales items on credit enter "75."

Days General A/P

How many days will you take to pay for non cost of sales items or services that you will buy on credit? (Range 0-90.) Enter 0 if you will not buy these items on credit.

Enter the average number of days that you will take to pay for non-cost of sales items or services that you buy on credit. Don't include in the average any items that you pay for in cash because cash purchases will be calculated separately.

S-T Interest Rate

What do you estimate your annual interest rate will be for short-term debt? (Range 0-100). Enter "0" if you will not have short-term debt.

Make your best estimate of what your bank or other lender will charge you for short-term loans. If you have no idea look in today's paper to find the current "prime rate" and add 2.00 percentage points to it. Bankers and equity lenders are very current with interest rates so if you must estimate, estimate slightly conservatively.

L-T Interest Rate

What do you estimate your annual interest rate will be for long-term debt? (Range 0-100). Enter "0" if you will not have long-term debt.

Make your best estimate of what your bank or other lender will charge you for long-term loans. If you have no idea look in today's paper to find the current "prime rate" and add 3.00 percentage points to it. Bankers and equity lenders are very current with interest rates so if you must estimate, estimate slightly conservatively.

Expense Headings

This list is the standard/default Expense headings for the Profit and Loss Projection. You may change these headings by typing a new heading (or leaving a blank) in place of the green-colored heading in the left hand column.

You can also make the entry appear blank by deleting it and not replacing it. This will "hide" the row on the Profit and Loss spreadsheet and will also return the formulas to their default value.

We have tried to make the standard/default headings as appropriate as possible for the vast majority of users. If the default headings are not appropriate for you, almost all of the headlines listed below may be changed to any other title you may choose. Simply type over the existing headline any new headline you would like to use.

A few special headlines, marked by an "*" can not be changed. The cells on these lines have special formulas that interact with other cells that would not be appropriate to re-name to other items. These rows may be deleted however by blanking them out.

In order to restore "*" deleted items the heading must be retyped **exactly** as originally listed. You may change headings such as General and Administrative, however if you delete these you will loose all sub-categories that fall below. Again be certain before proceeding with the deletion on major headings.

Comments

Comments are an important part of any business plan. Especially if you are seeking equity investment money we suggest that you consult with a qualified business attorney for specific advice on comments that should accompany financials (and your business plan as a whole) in your particular situation. In any event, comments are important to identify any major

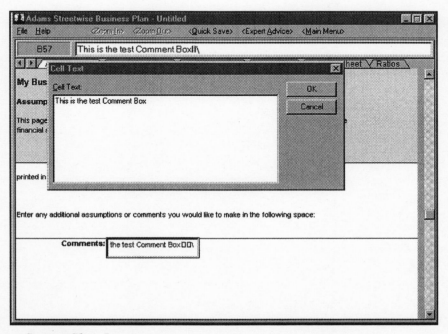

Screen Shot 5

assumptions not previously covered. Typical comments may include the following:

-All businesses have risks and hence their is no guarantee or assurance that the projections in these financials will be achieved.

-Sales projections are based upon the assumption of a __% market share

-Sales projections assume that the product will be completed by...

-Cost projections assume a ...% inflation rate

-Depreciation costs assume a weighted average depreciation schedule of .... years

-These projections assume that we will obtain $... in financing by....

To make typing a comment in the cell easier to see you may hit the F2 key to enlarge the cell into a more workable text box [see Screen Shot 5]. To create a large cell to work in you should double-click the F2 key.

STARTING BALANCE SHEET

About the starting balance sheet

The Starting Balance Sheet entries will be unique for every business and cannot be determined by formula's. Hence you must make all entries for the starting balance sheet--the software cannot determine any entries for you. [*See Screen Shot 6*].

Be sure that your total assets equal your total liabilities plus equity.

Basically the total liabilities and equity shows who has legal claim to the assets of the business. Hence the total liabilities and equity must always equal the total assets. And this is why a balance sheet is called a balance sheet.

Remember that a balance sheet is a snap shot of your business at one moment in time. This starting balance sheet should reflect your business at the date of the start of the business plan. Often the starting date on the business plan will be a future date. Hence the starting balance sheet will actually be a projection of what the starting balance sheet of the business will be on that future date.

Balance Sheet does not affect Profit and Loss Projection

The Starting Balance Sheet will not impact your profit and loss projection, but it will certainly impact your balance sheet projections and will generally impact your cash flow projections. So if you only want to prepare a profit and loss projection for your business, but no balance sheets or cash flows, then you could skip the starting balance sheet.

Screen Shot 6

Filling in the Starting Balance Sheet

Assets

Assets are anything that the business currently owns.

Current Assets

Current assets are assets that will be turned into cash within one year or may be converted to cash very quickly. Fixed assets such as equipment, buildings, machinery, etc. are not considered to be current assets even if you are planning to sell them in the near future.

Cash

Cash are your most liquid assets including checking accounts, money market funds, saving accounts.

Accounts receivable

Accounts receivable is money owed your business by customers as the result of regular business transactions. If you answered no to sales on credit in the Assumptions section your entry here should be 0. If this is not correct then return to Assumptions and correct your answer.

Inventory

Inventory includes finished goods, work in process, and raw material. If you entered 0 for cost of sales 0 must be your entry here, or if you entered 0 for days of inventory on hand enter 0 here.

Other current assets

Other current assets are all other current assets of the business. Examples to be included in this line include pre-paid rent, pre-paid taxes and pre-paid utilities.

Total current assets

Total current assets is calculated here by adding up cash, accounts receivable, inventory and other current assets.

Long term assets

Long term assets are assets that are not easily turned into cash, that typically have useful lives greater than one year. Examples are such items as equipment, buildings, land, motor vehicles, etc.

Depreciable assets

Depreciable assets are assets that depreciate over time such as equipment, motor vehicles, leasehold improvements and buildings. For this entry you should include your purchase price of the items, not their current market or book value.

Accumulated depreciation

This entry includes all of the depreciation accumulated to date on all of your depreciable assets. As depreciable assets get older they loose value. For example a 5 year old truck has less value than a brand new truck.

Depreciation is an accounting figure that records the deterioration in value of equipment, motor vehicles and buildings. Each of these items is assumed to loose a certain percentage of its value each year. Different accounting principles and tax laws apply to different categories of goods. For example you may be able to depreciate a car or truck over 3 years, a computer over 5 years, office furniture over 10 years, leasehold improvements over the life of the lease, buildings over 40 years.

So assuming that you are using simple straight-line depreciation, the matching monthly depreciation figures may be car or trucks: 1/36 of purchase price per month. For computers: 1/60 of purchase price per month. Office furniture: 1/120 per month. Buildings: 1/480 of purchase price per month.

Do not enter a negative number for accumulated depreciation as the spreadsheet is already formulated to subtract this item and a negative entry would result in the addition, not the subtraction of depreciation. Nor should you enter a percentage, this will result in erroneous data.

Net depreciable assets

Net depreciable assets is calculated by subtracting accumulated depreciation from depreciable assets.

Non-depreciable assets

Non depreciable assets are long-term assets that do not depreciate such as land.

Total long-term assets

Total long-term assets is calculated by adding up net depreciable assets and non-depreciable assets.

Total assets

Total assets is calculated by adding up total current assets and total long-term assets

Current liabilities

Current liabilities are liabilities that will be paid within one year.

Cost of sales payable

These are amounts that the business owes vendors for purchases of inventory or cost of sales items. This entry should be "0" if you answered no to Cost of Sales A/P on the assumption sheet.

Non-cost of sales payable

These are amounts that the business owes vendors for purchases of non-inventory/non-cost of sales items. This should be "0" if you answered no to Non Cost of Sales A/P on the Assumptions sheet.

Short-term debt

This is borrowed funds or notes that the business owes that are due within one year.

Income taxes due

This is all income taxes that the business owes. Sales taxes and any other taxes should be included elsewhere such as under non-cost of sales payables.

Because each business pays income taxes according to different schedules this program will not automatically pay off any income tax amount due. If you want to pay off income tax amounts due that exist on the Starting Balance you will have to overwrite the income tax entry on the Profit and Loss Statement spreadsheet.

Total current liabilities

This is the total of costs of sales payable, non cost of sales payable, short-term debt and income taxes due.

Long-term debt

This is borrowed funds or notes that the business owes that is due in more than one year.

Equity

Equity is the owner's or stockholder's net worth in the business.

Stock and paid-in capital

For a corporation or partnership this is the total amount of money that has been invested in the business, including the money to start your business plus any additional capital infusions you have made, not including re-investment of retained earnings.

For a sole proprietorship both the stock and paid-in capital entry and the retained earnings entry are better thought of as one entry "Net Worth." So to do financials for a sole proprietorship we would recommend setting stock and paid-in capital to zero and consider the retained earnings entry to reflect "Net Worth."

Retained earnings

Retained earnings are net income after tax that has not been distributed to the owner(s) of the business and instead has been kept in the business.

If you are not sure of what the retained earnings of your business is (or what your personal net worth is) you can calculate it by adding up all of your assets and subtracting all of your liabilities. This will give you your net worth or total equity. To determine retained earnings you would then subtract stock and paid-in capital from total equity.

Total equity

Total equity is the sum of stock and paid-in capital and retained earnings.

Total liabilities and equity

Total liabilities and equity is the sum of total liabilities plus total equity. This amount must equal total assets.

If these are not equal, carefully double check each entry for assets and liabilities. Then adjust the retained earnings entry so that total liabilities shows a total equal to total assets.

Do not proceed to the next part of the plan until the Starting Balance sheet "balances."

PROFIT AND LOSS PROJECTION

Profit and Loss Projection Overview

You will notice that when you first view the Profit and Loss Projection that a number of areas are already filled in. This is a result of the information you have already provided in the Assumptions and Starting Balance Sheet spreadsheets. There is however still more data to enter before your Profit and Loss Projection is finished. [*See Screen Shot 7*]

Data automatically fills to the right

Please note that the Profit and Loss Projection is set up to automatically fill from the left side to the right side of the page. So for example once you enter your starting month cost for insurance, it will automatically copy to all other months and be anualized into subsequent years of a multi-year plan.. Any of these automatically filled entries can be changed by typing new data into the appropriate cell.

Headings in left hand column

Most of the headings in the left hand column may be changed if you would like. Headings may not be changed directly on this page. Instead, select the Assumptions tab at the top of the spreadsheet to go to the Assumptions spreadsheet. Proceed to last assumption on the page to change headings on the Profit & Loss Projection.

If you have deleted any major heading, such as General and Administrative, subheadings will not appear on the spreadsheet. To restore the headings and subheads return to Assumptions and retype the heads exactly as they originally were.

Screen Shot 7

Starting date of plan

The starting date of the plan may be changed by going back to the Assumptions page and changing the starting date assumption.

Duration of plan

The duration of the plan may be either one year, two years, three years, four years or five years. All cases will include monthly detail for the first year only. To change the duration of the plan go back to the Assumptions page and change the duration of plan assumption. Changing the duration of the plan will have no effect on the formulas or calculations.

Filling in the Profit and Loss Projection

Sales

Sales should be entered in dollars (or whatever currency you are using), not in units. Sales should be net sales--in other words net sales after adjustments, any discounts, return, etc.

After you enter sales for the first month you will notice that it automatically carries the same value forward for additional months. If you want to enter different values for future months (or years) simply overwrite the automatically entered amount.

Cost of Sales

Cost of sales numbers should already appear on the Profit and Loss Projection. The numbers are determined by the Cost of Sales Percentage from the Assumptions page multiplied by the sales numbers. You can overwrite any Cost of Sales number, but you will also overwrite the formula.

Cost of sales are your direct costs of the materials or services that you have sold. For a manufacturing business you would include the costs of the product you are making. You will want to include all expenses that are related such as salaries of manufacturing personnel, raw materials, etc. For a retailer or wholesaler cost of sales is the cost you have incurred for products that you have actually sold - not the cost of products still in inventory.

For a service business cost of sales is your direct expenses of providing your service which would typically consist largely of labor costs--that is the labor costs of the people who are directly providing the service, not the support staff. For a restaurant, cost of sales is the cost of the food and beverages that you purchase.

Gross profit

Gross profit is calculated by subtracting cost of sales from sales. This number may not be over-written.

Gross profit margin

Gross profit divided by sales. This number may not be over-written. This ratio indicates the core profitability of the business versus sales before subtracting any of the marketing, sales, general and administrative costs of running the business. Like other profit margin ratio's, average and recommended gross profit margins will vary widely from one type of business to the next.

Marketing and Sales

Commissions

Commissions, if any, should already appear on the Profit and Loss Projection. The numbers are determined by the Commission Percentage from the Assumptions page multiplied by the sales numbers entered on this spreadsheet. You can overwrite any Commissions number, but you will also overwrite the formula. If don't have any Commissions you can just leave the entries blank or change the entries to 0.

Literature and Mailings

Include any coupons, brochures, direct mail pieces, catalogs, and other promotional material.

Advertising & Publicity

Include all advertising and publicity expenses, except those listed under other categories such as commissions or literature and mailings.

Other Marketing

All other marketing expenditures not covered in the above categories.

Total Marketing & Sales

Calculated by adding all marketing and sales costs. This number may not be overwritten.

General and Administrative (G&A)

Payroll

Gross payroll expenses. Note: if you have already counted some portion of payroll in cost of sales, do not double count it by including it here.

Payroll Taxes, Benefits

Payroll taxes, benefits should appear on the Profit and Loss Projection immediately as you enter the Payroll. The numbers are determined by the Payroll Tax Percentage from the Assumptions page multiplied by the Payroll.

Facilities & Equip./Rent

Includes rental and lease payments for facilities and equipment. This figure will usually remain the same throughout the year, unless you need to rent additional equipment, such as for a peak business period.

Maintenance & Repairs

Includes all maintenance and repair work and service contracts.

Utilities, Phone, Postage
Includes all utilities, phone, postage, courier expenses, internet access, etc.

Insurance
Include all insurance, except any insurance previously included under Payroll Taxes & Benefits.

Supplies
All the various supplies used in operating the business, except for items that directly become part of finished products or services (which would be included under cost of sales). Typical examples are office supplies, cleaning supplies, shipping materials, etc.

Freight
Freight costs, if any, should already appear on the Profit and Loss Projection. The number is determined by the Freight Costs from the Assumption page (entered as a percentage of sales) multiplied by the sales number. This number represents the cost of shipping or delivering your goods or products. You can overwrite Freight numbers, but you will also overwrite the formulas.

Auto, Travel & Entertainment
This category should include basically any local transportation of employees including auto mileage reimbursement, meals, overnight travel and entertainment expenses.

Legal & Accounting
Includes the fees you pay to external legal and accounting firms. In-house legal or accounting staff should be included in Payroll.

Other Outside Services
Includes cleaning services, landscaping, and all other outside services. You could also include temporary help firms and consultants in this category.

Misc. Taxes and Fees
All taxes and fees except income taxes. Examples include permits, licenses, real estate taxes, inventory taxes, etc.

Depreciation
Monthly portion of depreciation on capital equipment, motor vehicles, buildings and leasehold improvements. Most often this will remain constant over the course of the year.

Depreciation is an accounting figure that records the deterioration in value of equipment, motor vehicles and buildings. Each of these items is assumed to loose a certain percentage of its value each year. Different accounting principles and tax laws apply to different categories of goods. For example you may be able to depreciate a car or truck over 3 years, a computer over 5 years, office furniture over 10 years, leasehold improvements over the life of the lease, buildings over 40 years.

So assuming that you are using simple straight-line depreciation, the matching monthly depreciation figures may be car or trucks: 1/36 of purchase price per month. For computers: 1/60 of purchase price per month. Office furniture: 1/120 per month. Buildings: 1/480 of purchase price per month.

Check with your accountant or the IRS or the tax agency in your country to get the most appropriate depreciation figures for your situation.

Note that you must not enter a negative number. The program will automatically subtract the number you enter. Entering a negative will result in the addition of depreciation. Also do not enter a percentage as it will result in an error.

Other G&A Expenses
Includes all other operating costs except sales and marketing and cost of sales expenses. You should include a small amount for unforeseeable expenses or cost overruns.

Total G&A
Total of all general and administrative expenses.

Total Operating Costs
All general and administrative costs, marketing and sales costs and cost of sales.

Operating Profit
Sales less the total of cost of sales and total operating costs.

Operating Profit Margin
Operating profit divided by sales. This ratio indicates the profitability of operating the business versus sales before such costs as interest and taxes.

Non-Operating Costs
Costs that are not directly involved in the operation of the business such as interest expense.

Interest
The interest rate is automatically calculated for both short-term and long-term debt, and then added together to get the total for this entry. Interest expense will change when you change interest rate assumptions on the Assumptions spreadsheet, and when your amount of debt changes. You may change the amount of debt by adding or paying back debt on the Cash Flow Projection, or changing initial debt levels on the Starting Balance Sheet. If you overwrite the interest expense cells, you will lose the formulas in them and have to calculate interest manually.

Profit Before Income Taxes
Operating profit less non-operating costs.

Pre-Tax Profit Margin

Profit before income taxes divided by sales. This ratio indicates the profitability of the business versus sales after deducting all costs of operating the business except income taxes.

Income Taxes

All federal, state and local income taxes that may apply.

Income tax numbers should already appear on the Profit and Loss Projection. The numbers are determined by the Income Tax Percentage from the Assumptions page multiplied by the Profit Before Income Taxes. You can overwrite any Income Tax number, but you will also over-ride the formula.

Note that income taxes are shown monthly, because income taxes are an on-going expense of running a business even though smaller businesses may only have to pay income taxes quarterly for example.

This spreadsheet allows the Income Tax figures to flow negative if the Profit Before Income Tax is negative. If you have profit in some months and losses in other months, the negative income tax figures will be added against the positive income tax figures over the course of the year. If your overall year shows a loss, you will show a negative Income Tax entry. A business entity may either be able to get at least a partial income tax refund if they show a loss or a tax loss carry forward. Ask your accountant for advice on your specific situation.

Net Profit

Net profit after all expenses, including income taxes.

Net Profit Margin

Net Profit divided by sales. This ratio indicates the overall profitability of the business versus sales.

CASH FLOW PROJECTION

Cash Flow Overview

You will notice that when you first view the Cash Flow Projection that many of the cells are already filled in. This is a result of information you have already provided in the Assumptions, Starting Balance Sheet, and Profit and Loss Projection spreadsheets. For many users there may be no additional information that needs to be added at this point. Check the help instruction for each row carefully to determine if you should add more data. [*See Screen Shot 8*].

Changing Automatically Calculated Entries

Most users will want to carefully avoid changing the pre-calculated entries. However, to make this spreadsheet more versatile for power users, most of the pre-calculated entries may be changed if you need to. If you do change pre-calculated entries be aware that you are overwriting formulas and that your new data will not match the data on the accompanying spreadsheets.

As a safeguard against accidentally overwriting a formula a warning message will alert you before allowing you to proceed. This will appear each time and may not be turned off.

Lawn Masters of Newton
Cash Flow Projection

	Jan-1998	Feb-1998	Mar-1998	Apr-1998	May-1998	Jun-1998	Jul-1998	Aug
Starting Cash	22,330	46,593	82,418	181,772	217,817	246,408	262,967	31
Sources								
Cash Sales	36,000	75,000	225,000	305,000	305,000	305,000	300,000	26
Credit Sales	0	0	0	0	0	0	0	
Short-Term Loan Proceeds	0	0	0	0	0	0	0	
Long-Term Loan Proceeds	0	175,000	0	0	0	0	0	
Equity Capital Proceeds	0	0	0	0	0	0	0	
Total Sources	36,000	250,000	225,000	305,000	305,000	305,000	300,000	26
Uses								
Cost of Sales / Inventory	0	0	0	0	0	0	0	
Payroll & Related	7,910	10,735	72,320	122,040	122,040	122,040	122,040	12
Non-Payroll Expenses	3,200	22,300	43,300	128,900	136,300	136,100	101,100	10
Interest	0	1,604	1,577	1,551	1,524	1,497	1,470	
Purchase Depreciable Assets	0	175,000	0	0	0	0	0	
Purchase Non-Dep. Assets	0	0	0	0	0	0	0	
Dividends, Owner Pay-Outs	0	0	0	0	0	0	0	
Short-Term Debt Payments	0	0	0	0	0	0	0	

Screen Shot 8

Filling in the Cash Flow Projection

Starting Cash

You should not change the starting cash balance items on the cash flow. Starting cash for one period is the same as the ending cash position from the previous period, except for the first starting cash position, which is the same as the starting cash on your Starting Balance Sheet.

Sources

These items show the sources that your business will receive cash from.

Cash sales

You should not change items in this row. This row shows the cash your business will receive from sales made for cash. The data is determined by your sales estimate from the Profit and Loss Projection and the credit sales percentage from the Assumptions spreadsheet.

Credit sales

You should not change items in this row. This row shows the cash your business will receive from credit sales. It is determined by the your sales estimate from the Profit and Loss Projection, the credit sales % and the days credit from the Assumptions, and from any accounts receivable on the Starting Balance Sheet.

Short-term loan proceeds

Enter proceeds from any short-term loans in this row. You should enter enough proceeds from short-term loans so that the cash flow at the end of the month and each year reflects a positive balance. Generally you should enter items in this row, only after you have completed any other entries to be made on this page. This will make it easier to determine the appropriate level of short-term borrowing that you may need.

Once you have entered short-term loan proceeds you need to recheck your cash flow at the end of each month. You will notice that it changed because your cash use for interest was automatically recalculated. It is likely that you will have to increase your short-term loan proceeds further to cover increased interest costs. Especially if you are running your business with small cash balances, you may have to add to short-term loan proceeds several times to have a positive cash flow at the end of each month.

Also don't forget to enter repayments of short-term debt in the Uses section. If you are unable to payback short-term debt quickly, then you need to consider other financing options such as long-term debt or additional equity investments.

If any loan proceeds that you receive have been discounted for pre-paid interest, add the interest to the net proceeds to obtain the full or gross amount of the loan, and enter that amount here. The interest will be automatically calculated.

Long-term loan proceeds

Enter proceeds from any long-term loans in this row. As with short-term loan proceeds, you can increase long-term loan proceeds to help finance your business. However, short-term swings in financing needs (such as swings within any 12 month period) should be covered by short-term debt.

Equity capital proceeds

Enter proceeds from any new equity infusions in this row, such as if a new or current investor contributes an additional amount of money to the business.

Total sources

This row totals all of your sources of cash from all sources.

Uses

These items show all of the ways that the business will use cash.

Cost of sales

You should not change items in this row. This row shows when you will pay for cost of sales items (or inventory).

The entries in this row have been calculated based upon many factors including: sales and cost of sales from the Profit and Loss Projection, cost of sales accounts payable and inventory from the Starting Balance Sheet and days inventory, cost of sales, cost of sales accounts payable and cost of sales accounts payable percentage and days cost of sales accounts payable from the Assumptions.

Payroll & Related

You should not change items in this row. This row shows when you will pay for payroll and payroll taxes/benefits. The items in this row are from payroll and payroll taxes/benefits from the Profit and Loss Projection.

We have assumed that you will pay for these items on a cash basis. In reality your business like most firms probably pays payroll a few days after the payroll period ends, and pays payroll taxes a few days or even a few weeks after they are incurred. However, it is a close enough estimate and perfectly acceptable to consider payroll and payroll related items a cash, not a credit, expense for the purpose of projecting cash flow.

Non-Payroll Expenses

You should not change items in this row. This row shows when you will pay for non-payroll expenses excluding cost of sales items and interest and income taxes.

The items in this row are calculated from the expense items in the Profit and Loss Projection, the non cost of sales payables from the Starting Balance Sheet and the general accounts payable percentage and days general accounts payable from the Assumptions spreadsheet.

Interest

You should not change items in this row. Interest is taken from the Profit and Loss Projection and assumed to be paid on a cash basis. Interest will change when you change your level of debt or your interest rate assumptions.

Purchase depreciable assets

Enter the full purchase cost of depreciable assets purchased during each period in this row. Examples include equipment, motor vehicles, leasehold improvements and buildings.

Purchase non-depreciable assets

Enter the full purchase cost of any non-depreciable assets purchased during each period in this row. Land is an example of a non-depreciable asset.

Dividends, owner pay-outs

Enter any dividends or pay-outs to owners in this row.

Short-term debt payments

Enter any payments of principal of short-term debt in this row. Interest payments should not be included here, these are automatically calculated on the Profit and Loss Projection under interest. The resulting entry also carries forward to the interest line on the Cash Flow Projection.

Long-term debt payments

Enter any payments of principal of long-term debt in this row. Interest payments should not be included here, these are automatically calculated on the Profit and Loss Projection under interest. The resulting entry also carries forward to the interest line on the Cash Flow Projection.

Total uses before taxes

This row totals all of your uses of cash before income taxes.

Income taxes.

This row shows when you will pay income taxes. It is pre-determined from the income tax entry on the Profit and Loss Projection. Timing of income taxes differs some from one company to the next and from one country and state to the next. The timing of your income taxes may be different than indicated here.

I would recommend that you don't change the projected income tax payment schedule here because you will have to over-ride formulas and erase the interactivity between the different spreadsheets. Also by estimating payment of income taxes monthly you are erring on the side of caution. But if you really want to, you can over-write the projected income tax payments--make sure you make appropriate changes on the Balance Sheet Projection and Profit and Loss Projection.

Note : This row does not automatically pay income taxes due from the Starting Balance sheet. To pay income taxes from the Starting Balance sheet you must overwrite the cell for the appropriate month that you wish to pay the taxes

Total uses after taxes

This row totals all of your uses of cash including income taxes.

Net change in cash

This row reflects the change in your cash position during the month. It is determined by subtracting all cash uses during the period from all cash sources.

Ending cash position

This row reflects the amount of cash that you will have on hand at the end of the period. It is determined by adding the Starting cash to the Net change in cash. The ending cash position for one period is the same as the starting cash for the following period.

This page intentionally blank.

BALANCE SHEET PROJECTION

Do not make changes on the Balance Sheet Projection unless you are extremely confident in you abilities with spreadsheets and thoroughly understand accounting formulas.

If you are working on the spreadsheets in the proper order, all appropriate items on the Balance Sheet Projection are already filled in and you should not make any changes on it.

The Balance Sheet fills in as a result of the information that you should have already provided in the Assumptions, Starting Balance Sheet, Profit and Loss Projection and Cash Flow Projection.

It may be possible that some entire rows on the Balance Sheet Projection are 0. But they should be 0 if you have already properly filled in the other spreadsheets. For example, if you don't have inventory, the inventory row should be all 0's. [*See Screen Shot 9*]

Changing Automatically Calculated Entries

Most users will want to avoid any changes at all to the pre-calculated entries on the Balance Sheet-- and on the Balance Sheet all of the entries are pre-calculated. However, to make this spreadsheet more versatile for power users, most of the pre-calculated entries may be changed if you need to. If you do change pre-calculated entries be aware that you are overwriting formulas and that your new data will not match the data on the accompanying spreadsheets.

Period Ending:	Jan-1998	Feb-1998	Mar-1998	Apr-1998	May-1998	Jun-1998	Jul-1998
Assets							
Current assets							
Cash	46,593	82,418	181,772	217,817	246,408	262,967	311,293
Accounts Receivable	0	0	0	0	0	0	0
Inventory	0	0	0	0	0	0	0
Other Current Assets	1,200	1,200	1,200	1,200	1,200	1,200	1,200
Total Current Assets	47,793	83,618	182,972	219,017	247,608	264,167	312,493
Long-Term Assets							
Depreciable Assets	78,400	253,400	253,400	253,400	253,400	253,400	253,400
Accumulated Depreciation	29,300	35,700	42,100	48,500	54,900	61,300	67,700
Net Depreciable Assets	49,100	217,700	211,300	204,900	198,500	192,100	185,700
Non-Depreciable Assets	0	0	0	0	0	0	0
Total Long-Term Assets	49,100	217,700	211,300	204,900	198,500	192,100	185,700
Total Assets	96,893	301,318	394,272	423,917	446,108	456,267	498,193
Liabilities & Equity							
Current Liabilities							

Screen Shot 9

Categories on the Balance Sheet Projection

Assets

Assets are anything that the business currently owns.

Current Assets

Current assets are assets that will be turned into cash within one year or may be converted to cash very quickly. Fixed assets such as equipment, buildings, machinery, etc. are not considered to be current assets even if you are planning to sell them in the near future.

Cash

Cash are your most liquid assets including checking accounts, money market funds, saving accounts.

Accounts receivable

Accounts receivable is money owed your business by customers as the result of regular business transactions (i.e. excluding any special loans or financing you may have arranged for customers).

Inventory

Inventory includes finished goods, work in process, and raw material.

Other current assets

Other current assets are all other current assets of the business. Examples to be included in this line include pre-paid rent, pre-paid taxes and pre-paid utilities.

Total current assets

Total current assets is calculated here by adding up cash, accounts receivable, inventory and other current assets.

Long term assets

Long term assets are assets that are not easily turned into cash and typically include such items as equipment, buildings, land, motor vehicles, etc.

Depreciable assets

Depreciable assets are assets that depreciate over time such as equipment, motor vehicles, leasehold improvements and buildings. For this entry you should include your purchase price of the items, not their current market or book value.

Accumulated depreciation

This entry includes all of the depreciation accumulated to date on all of your depreciable assets. It is calculated by adding depreciation from the profit and loss statements to the starting accumulated depreciation on the starting balance sheet.

Net depreciable assets

Net depreciable assets is calculated by subtracting accumulated depreciation from depreciable assets.

Non-depreciable assets

Non depreciable assets are long-term assets that do not depreciate such as land.

Total long-term assets

Total long-term assets is calculated by adding up net depreciable assets and non-depreciable assets.

Total assets

Total assets is calculated by adding up total current assets and total long-term assets

Liabilities and Equity

Liabilities and equity shows who has claims to the business assets.

Current liabilities

Current liabilities are liabilities that will be paid within one year.

Short-term debt

This is borrowed funds or notes that the business owes that is due within one year. This is calculated by taking the starting short-term debt from the starting balance sheet, adding in short-term loan proceeds and subtracting short-term debt payments from the cash flow.

Cost of sales payable

These are amounts that the business owes vendors for purchases of inventory or cost of sales items.

Non cost of sales payable

These are amounts that the business owes vendors for purchases of non inventory/non cost of sales items.

Income taxes due

This is all income taxes that the business owes.

Total current liabilities

This is the total of costs of sales payable, non cost of sales payable, short-term debt and income taxes due.

Long-term debt

This is borrowed funds or notes that the business owes that are due in more than one year.

Equity

Equity is the owner's net worth in the business.

Stock and paid-in capital

For a corporation or partnership this is the total amount of money that has been invested in the business, including the money to start your business plus any additional capital infusions you have made, not included re-investment of retained earnings.

For a sole proprietorship both the stock and paid-in capital entry and the retained earnings entry are better thought of as one entry "Net Worth." So to do financials for a sole proprietorship we would recommend setting stock and paid-in capital to zero and consider the retained earnings entry to reflect "Net Worth."

Retained earnings

Retained earnings are net income after tax that has not been distributed to the owner(s) of the business and instead has been kept in the business.

If you are not sure of what the retained earnings of your business is (or what your personal net worth is) you can calculate it by adding up all of your assets and subtracting all of your liabilities. This will give you your net worth or total equity. To determine retained earnings you would then subtract stock and paid-in capital from total equity.

Total equity

Total equity is the sum of stock and paid-in capital and retained earnings.

Total liabilities and equity

Total liabilities and equity is the sum of total liabilities plus total equity. This amount must equal total assets.

KEY RATIOS AND ANALYSIS

Do not make changes on the Key Ratios and Analysis

Don't make changes to this sheet unless you are extremely confident in you abilities with spreadsheets and thoroughly understand accounting formulas.

This should be the last spreadsheet that you review and all appropriate items on this spreadsheet are already filled in and you should not make any changes on it. Key ratios and analysis are derived from your Assumptions information and the information you input on the other Financial Spreadsheets.

Overwriting will loose the formulas

You can overwrite the information here, but if you do so you will lose the formula for this datasheet. The only way to get the formula back would be to start a new spreadsheet. (Unless you have previously saved another set of your data under a different file name). So we suggest that before your overwrite any formula on this page, you save your work under a different file name, using the "Save As" command in the file menu.

Adams Streetwise Business Plan - C:\Program Files\Adams\ASWBP\Data\Lawn_11.vts

File Help   <Zoom In> <Zoom Out>   <Quick Save> <Expert Advice> <Main Menu>

Assumptions ∨ Starting Balance ∨ Profit and Loss ∨ Cash Flow ∨ Balance Sheet ∨ Ratios

Lawn Masters of Newton
Ratios and Analysis

	Jan-1998	Feb-1998	Mar-1998	Apr-1998	May-1998	Jun-1998	Jul-1998	Aug-199
Quick Ratio	2.14	1.93	1.42	1.61	1.82	2.61	3.09	3.4
Current Ratio	2.14	1.93	1.42	1.61	1.82	2.61	3.09	3.4
Debt to Equity Ratio	0.30	2.63	3.23	2.58	2.10	1.38	1.10	0.9
Debt to Assets Ratio	0.23	0.72	0.76	0.72	0.68	0.58	0.52	0.4
Return on Equity Ratio	0.02	0.10	0.11	0.21	0.18	0.25	0.19	0.1
Return on Assets Ratio	0.01	0.03	0.03	0.06	0.06	0.11	0.09	0.0
Sales Break Even	34210	60435	207620	264740	264540	229540	229540	22954
Working Capital	25493	49318	54072	82717	111508	163067	211393	24998

Screen Shot 10

Profitability versus sales ratios

Profitability versus sales ratios are included on the Profit and Loss Projection spreadsheet. Desirable and average profitability ratios will vary widely by type of business.

Here are the key ratios and financial analysis and the formulas that are used to derive them:

Quick Ratio:

(Current Assets - Inventory) / Current Liabilities

Also called the Acid Test, this ratio should usually be greater than one. The ratio tests the very short-term liquidity versus current obligations of the business. Inventory is not included because it is assumed that inventory can not be as quickly turned into cash as other current assets such as bank accounts and accounts receivable.

Current Ratio:

Current Assets / Current Liabilities

This ratio should usually be greater than two. This ratio tests the short-term liquidity of the business.

Debt to Equity Ratio:

Total Liabilities / Total Equity

This ratio should usually be one or less, but benchmarks for this ratio vary considerably among different industries. This ratio indicates how heavy the debt load of the business is versus the equity. A high debt to equity ratio may indicate the business may be considered by potential lenders to be at its debt capacity and too risky a candidate for additional debt financing.

Debt to Assets Ratio:

Total Liabilities / Total Assets

This ratio should be .5 or less, but benchmarks for this ratio vary considerably among different industries. This ratio is almost identical to the debt to equity ratio, except that the debt load is compared to assets plus equity, instead of just equity.

Return on Equity Ratio:

Net Profit / Total Equity

This ratio should be high enough to make it worthwhile for investors to make equity investments in the business. This ratio should reflect an expected return high enough to offset risks of the investment. Because virtually all new and/or small businesses have a lot of risks, investors expect to earn much higher returns than if they invested in larger, more stable businesses.

Return on Assets Ratio:

Net Profit / Total Assets

This ratio shows how effectively the business uses it's total assets in earning net profits. This ratio should at least be significantly higher than the highest interest rate the firm will be paying on its debt financing.

Sales Break Even:

Fixed Costs / (1 - (cost of goods % + commission % + freight %))

This value indicates the amount of sales that you need to achieve to reach break-even. Your break-even level should be significantly lower than your most likely sales projection. Cost of goods sold, commissions and freight are all costs that vary with sales. For this formula these variable costs are taken from the Assumptions values that you assigned, even if have overwritten them in the Profit and Loss Projection.

Working Capital:

(Current Assets - Current Liabilities)

Working capital measures the amount of funds that the business has available to pay for the daily operations of the business. This number should be positive and should be large enough to easily cover the expected ebbs and flows of running the business.

Alternative Calculation Method

For several of the above ratio's (Debt to Equity Ratio, Debt to Assets Ratio, Return on Equity Ratio, Return on Total Assets Ratio), there is an alternative, slightly more complex, method than we have used for the calculation. For our calculations we have used the equity or assets at the end of the period, as reflected on the balance sheet. Instead, you could determine these ratio's using the average equity or assets employed during the period. To determine the average equity or assets employed you take the starting amount and the ending amount and divide by 2. However, it is very unlikely that any potential banker or investor will ask you refine these ratio's.

Annualizing Returns

For use of capital ratio's (Return on Equity Ratio, Return on Total Assets Ratio) we have used the return for each period shown. In other words the return in each monthly column is on a monthly basis, whereas the return for each year is on an annual basis. As an alternative you could annualize the monthly return ratio's by multiplying them by 12. So a return that may currently show 1% per month, would instead show 12% per year.

This page intentionally blank.

USING COMPLETE BUSINESS PLAN TEXT

Virtually everything on the CD used to create a business plan is also provided for you in this manual so that you can use them both more effectively. We will walk you through each step of creating business plan in order. All of the text options for a given section will be presented in this manual. Obviously you would not use every selection in your plan but the more choices available to you the more likely it is that you will find one that closely fits your needs.

For those needing a little help navigating the program, each section with begin with a segment called "How Do I Get Here?" This feature will be framed and centered on the page (see below for example). It may also include a screen shot and instruction on how to access the particular element of Complete Business Plan.

How Do I Get Here?
From the **Main Menu** click on the Business Plan icon. Select Business Plan Text and click OK. You will then be given the option of working on and existing business plan or starting a new one, select the appropriate option and click OK. [If you choose to work on an existing plan the Open dialog box will appear. Click on the plan you want to work on and then click on the Open button.]

Although this manual is presented in order you can, if you prefer, start in the middle, simply go to that section and begin. Also, if you want to go back and change or update a section of your business plan there is no need to start from the beginning, simply choose that section, edit what you need and save it. The rest of your plan will remain unchanged.

Understanding that some people learn better by example, we are also providing a business plan for a fictitious company called "Lawn Masters of Newton." Within each category you will find a boxed off section with the corresponding section of "Lawn Masters" plan.

Summary

How Do I Get Here?

From the **Main Menu** click on the Business Plan icon. Select Business Plan Text and click OK. You will then be given the option of working on and existing business plan or starting a new one, select the appropriate option and click OK. [If you choose to work on an existing plan the Open dialog box will appear. Click on the plan you want to work on and then click on the Open button.]

The Business Plan window is now visible (see screen shot 1, next page) with your text options in the top half view and your work area below. Click on Summary on the sub-menu bar and the summary text will appear. Double click to select a paragraph from the preformatted text. To edit the text click on the text in the bottom window at the point you wish to edit. All common Windows editing functions are available.

The summary needs to be brief (not more than one or two pages) and highly focused. It needs to succinctly build a basic understanding of the company's business concept, the current situation, the key success factors, and the overall financial picture. If the purpose of your business plan is to attract financing, then you've got to grab the reader's attention right away. There are plenty of opportunities available for investors and lenders, so you'll need to convince them at a quick first impression that your business is worth some careful consideration [See Screen Shot 11].

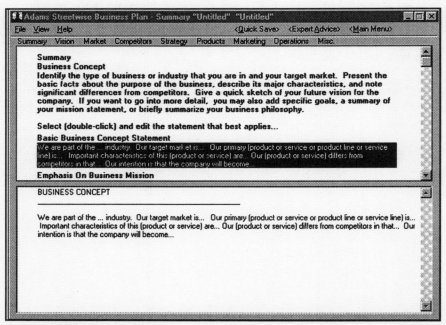

Screen Shot 2

Business Concept

Identify your industry and very briefly describe what your business does. Present the basic facts about the purpose of the business and describe its major characteristics. You could also note any fundamental differences between your business and other firms in the industry.

Select and edit the statement that best applies....

Basic business concept statement

We are part of the ... industry. Our target market is... Our primary (product or service or product line or service line) is... Important characteristics of this (product or service) are... Our (product or service) differs from competitors in that... Our intention is that the company will become...[*See Business Plan Example #1*]

Emphasis on business mission

We (produce or provide) (describe product or service). The mission of our business is to (produce products or deliver services) that (deliver superior value, offer outstanding quality, offer the best price, are the most technologically advanced, provide highly personalized solutions, specifically designed for the needs of.., are individually tailored for the needs of each customer, for a specific market niche..., will build a brand name franchise, will lead their markets, are the most innovative in the industry, are professional in every way, etc.). . We intend to fulfill this mission by giving extra effort to (customer service, sales, engineering, production, research, customer's needs, changes in the market, superior workmanship, customer satisfaction, addressing customer needs, etc.)

Responding to new needs

In the (relevant field) industry today, there is a much greater awareness than ever before of the need for (new needs in the relevant field). This has occurred as a result of (changes in the field), and creates tremendous opportunities for businesses that specifically respond to this situation. We intend to distinguish ourselves from the competition by offering (high quality, superior, technically advanced, state-of-the-art, highly personalized, highly customized, high performance, guaranteed, etc.) (products or services) which address these new needs much more effectively than current companies in our market area.

Entering a fast growing industry

The (industry) industry has expanded rapidly in the past several years and growth is expected to continue at a strong pace for the foreseeable future. This offers excellent opportunities for new companies to enter this market. We intend to address the needs of customers in this market who seek... We will address this need by providing... Distinguishing characteristics of our (business or product(s) or service(s) will be...

Expansion of existing service business

We have been successful in providing (type of) services, with a special emphasis on (area of specialization). We have an excellent reputation and are best known for our (specific service characteristic), which differentiates us from our competitors. The company is profitable and has great potential for growth and for becoming a market leader. To best take advantage of our growth opportunities, the company would like to (new developments or expenses that financing is required for). These expenditures will allow us to finance and support our planned growth, without sacrificing the quality of service for which we are known. [*See Business Plan Example #1*]

Become a market leader

Our goal is to become one of the leading (type of business) in the (geographical area). We intend to accomplish this goal by offering a set of (products/services) that meet client needs better than any competitor by (utilization of state of the art technology, building a superior workforce through careful hiring and continuous training and development, closely meeting the needs of each customer, by differentiating our products by..., by offering superior service) We will also create a high level of visibility and awareness for our (products/services) by a consistent and carefully targeted marketing strategy.

Lawn Masters of Newton

Business Plan Example #1

Business Concept

Lawn Masters of Newton is part of the lawn maintenance industry. Our target market is homeowners in the Newton, Massachusetts community. Our principal service is lawn care, including seeding, fertilizing, mowing, and shrubbery and tree care. Our service differs from competitors in that we offer a complete set of services offered on an a la carte basis. Our intention is that the company will become the leading provider of lawn maintenance services in Newton.

We have been successful in providing lawn maintenance services, with a special emphasis on one-stop shopping. We have an excellent reputation and are best known for our customer service and flexibility, which differentiates us from our competitors. The company is profitable and has great potential for growth and for becoming a leader in the local market area. To best take advantage of our growth opportunities, the company would like to purchase new maintenance equipment and move to a larger facility. These expenditures will allow us to finance and support our planned growth, without sacrificing the quality of service that we are known for.

In this section note that the text has been altered to fit "Lawn Masters'" specific goals.

Change of strategic direction

The company was formed in (Year) to (initial purpose). Historically, the target market for our (products or services) has been (target market), which we have reached through a variety of advertising and publicity channels. However, at this point in time, due to significant changes in the field, including (indicate changes), a new strategic direction is warranted. We now plan to shift our focus to (new target market.) We expect to maintain some of the current (products or services), but also to add new (products or services) such as...

Current Situation

The nature of this section will depend somewhat on the status of your business and your purpose for writing this plan. If you are a start-up for example, you will probably want to describe the stage the company is at now. Has the company had any sales yet? Is all the staff hired? Is the product or service concept finalized? If it's an existing company, you might want to start by telling how long the firm has been in business. Is the situation stable? How consistent are sales and profits? How does it compare to other firms in the industry? What are the major challenges or opportunities facing the firm?

Select and edit the statement that best applies....

Basic current situation statement

The company was founded as a (sole proprietorship, partnership, corporation, S corporation, limited liability company) in (location) on (date). Currently the company is (well established in its market, becoming established in its market, highly profitable, profitable, in a start-up mode, about to ship its first product, ready to begin operations, seeking money to begin operations, seeking seed money, etc.) The major challenge(s) the firm is facing at this point is (are)... It intends to respond to it (them) by... The major opportunity(ies) available to the firm is (are)... The firm intends to take advantage of it (them) by...[*See Business Plan Example #2*]

Start-up company

We are a start-up, incorporated in (Year) in the State of (State). The principal owners are (Name), whose title is (Title); (Name), whose title is (Title), and (Name), whose title is (Title). Other key personnel include (Name), (Name), and (Name), who bring special expertise in the areas of (area), (area), and (area) respectively. With this team of experienced and talented individuals, the company will be positioned to meet an emerging, under-served need for (need to focus on). We are currently (in the initial planning stage, in the research and development stage, about to finish plans for our first product, finalizing plans for our operation, about to make firm commitments to begin operations, ready to begin production, seeking seed money..., seeking additional capital to...) The major challenges we face before beginning operations are... We hope to begin business by...

Existing business

We have been in business for ... years with sales in our past fiscal year ending (date) reaching... In recent years our sales have been (growing rapidly, growing moderately, growing slowly, growing steadily, growing, stable, flat, declining slightly, declining, erratic). Recently we have been (highly profitable, profitable, moderately profitable, marginally profitable, at break-even in terms of profits, nearing break-even, experiencing slight losses, experiencing losses, performing erratically in terms of profitability.) Factors influencing our recent performance include... Upcoming challenges that we face include... We intend to meet these challenges by... The largest opportunity(ies) that we face is (are)... We hope to take advantage of this opportunity by...

Existing business facing changing market

Our company was formed in (Year) as a (form of business) under the laws of the State of (State). We have seen massive changes in our industry in recent years. New technologies, increased consumer awareness, and global competitive pressures are largely responsible for these changes, and for many companies providing (products/services) in this marketplace, it has been a challenging time.

Competition has been fierce, product life cycles have been shortening, market shares have been changing rapidly, profitability for many firms have been erratic and some players have experienced severe financial problems. We have survived in this difficult atmosphere, but challenges remain. The most pressing challenge facing us is... We intend to face this by... Other important issues we face are...

At the same time the market is very large and a successful player in this industry can potentially enjoy high profitability.

Innovative new business

While the (relevant industry) field is currently dominated by a few large companies, our research shows that the situation is ripe for a new company with a new approach. We believe we can successfully enter the market by offering (products or services) that (describe unique benefit of your product or service). This differs from current (products or services) in that... We believe that buyers will find the competitive benefit of our (products or services) compelling enough that we will be able to build sales quickly and establish a solid market posi-

---

Lawn Masters of Newton

Business Plan Example #2

Current Situation

The company was founded as a corporation in the Commonwealth of Massachusetts on April 1, 1986. Currently the company is well established in its market, with sales in our past fiscal year reaching $1,350,000. In recent years our sales have been growing steadily. The major challenge the firm is facing at this point is expansion in order to increase market share. It intends to respond to this challenge by purchasing new equipment so that we are able to put more teams in the field, by moving to a larger facility, and by launching several innovative marketing and publicity efforts.

In the next few years, it is estimated that lawn maintenance services in Newton, Massachusetts will grow by at least 10 - 20%. This growth will be driven by the aging of the population base, the increasing value of residential property in Newton, and the robust overall economic situation in New England. We know that we are not the only company to see the business opportunities created by this expected growth, but we do feel that our one-stop, menu-oriented service structure is a unique response to the situation that will help us stand out in what will be a crowded marketplace.

tion. We have (performed market surveys, spoken with prospective customers, studied historical market research, spoken with retailers, spoken with sales people, done focus groups, observed the success of a similar business approach in other markets) to confirm that customers are interested in our new approach. A summary of our (interviews with prospective buyers, our market research, our telephone survey, discussions with retailers, findings from relevant industry studies) is included at the end of this business plan.

Growing business

(Company name) is a (# of)-year old business, operating in the State of (State) at (business location). There are (# of) current owners: (Name) owns (%) of the outstanding stock, (Name) owns (%), and (Name) owns (%). In the last complete fiscal year, the Company had gross revenues of ($) and total operating expenses of ($), for a net profit of ($). Projections for the current fiscal year show a (%) growth in net profits. In the next few years, it is estimated that our segment of the (relevant industry) industry will also grow by at least (%). This growth will be driven by (growth factor), (growth factor), and (growth factor). We know that we are not the only company to see the business opportunities created by this expected growth, but we do feel that our (type of) (product/service) is a unique response to the situation that will help us stand out in what will be a crowded marketplace.

Ready to expand and move out of home office

The company was founded as a (sole proprietorship, partnership, corporation, limited liability company) in (date). The principle owner(s) is (are) ... with ...% ownership. ...is also the founder and CEO. To date the business has been operated from the founder's residence in (location). At this point the business is ready to step up it's level of business activity, including moving to a commercial facility. The company plans to (buy, lease, sub-lease, rent) approximately ...feet of (grade A office space, office space, industrial space, warehouse space, retail space, space that is suitable for...). The company also plans to hire...additional people, primarily in (function) positions. While sales last year were $..., they have been gaining momentum, and sales this year are expected to reach $... The company expects to expand largely by (increasing its customer base, finding new customers, adding new products, adding new services, increasing revenues with current customers, entering new markets, expanding our target market to...).

Seeking initial investors or partners

At this point, we have refined our business concept and developed an extensive plan for taking this concept to market. We are now seeking initial equity investors or partners.

Seed money in place

(Company name) has raised ($) through the company founders and other private sources. The breakdown of initial investment by source is as follows...These funds have been utilized to (uses of seed funds), which is proceeding successfully at this time. When the remaining capital requirements have been met, (object of seed funds) will already be complete, and the Company will be able to focus on (next objectives).

Purpose of creating this plan

The purpose of writing this business plan is to (attract additional equity investment, obtain a bank loan, establish a line of credit, secure financing, re-evaluate our entire business, develop an overall business strategy, establish better control and direction of the business, correct the following problems..., address the following issues...). Specifically what we would like to accomplish is... The current situation has come about because...

Key Success Factors

Explain the factors that will help insure that your business will be successful. Is it a new business? What has been responsible for your success to date if you are an established business.. What is your real strength, your ace in the hole?

Select and edit the one or two statements that best apply....

Key success factors statement

The success of our business (has been, is, will be) largely a result of (superior products, superior service, extra attention to detail throughout our operation, our ability to deliver state of the art products or services, the unique talents of our key personnel, a highly experienced and adept core group of employees, a loyal and dedicated staff, our ability to successfully differentiate our products or services from the competition, our ability to successfully compete on price by rigorously controlling costs, an aggressive sales effort, highly targeted marketing, compelling advertising, our strategy to target a specific market niche..., our decision to focus on customers who...). In particular what really sets us apart from the competition is... This translates into a benefit for customers because...[*See Business Plan Example #3*]

Key success factors listed in order of importance

There are several key factors that can be identified as being particularly important in our firm's (ability to succeed, success to date). In order of relative importance these factors are:
1. (Success factor #1)
2. (Success factor #2)
3. (Success factor #3)
4. (Success factor #4)

Management team

Our major asset is our highly talented and experienced management team. The (# of) individuals complement each other well, combining backgrounds in a diverse group of important areas. (Key person #1) brings expertise in... (Key person #2) brings expertise in... (Key person #3) brings.... Together, these strengths cover many major operational aspects of the business with solid experience and a proven record of success. (Refer to the resumes at the end of the business plan for more information). [*See Business Plan Example #3*]

Reputation and contacts in the industry

While our company has not yet registered any sales, we have a terrific reputation and a wealth of important contacts in the industry because of the key people already (on board, hired, involved in the business as an employee or investor). These individuals will help us to attract top employees for other positions that remain to be filled, will help us get in the door at major customers, will help us generate visibility in the media, and will generally lend a level of instant credibility to our entire business. Here is a summary list of key hire to date and a brief summary of their background. (For more information see their resumes at the end of this business plan:

(Key person #1)   (...years of experience in... at...)
(Key person #1)   (...years of experience in... at...)
(Key person #1)   (...years of experience in... at...)

Lawn Masters of Newton

Business Plan Example #3

Key Success Factors

The success of our business has been and will continue to be largely a result of our ability to deliver dependable, high quality lawn maintenance services custom tailored to each customer's needs.

More specifically, the key factors that can be identified as being particularly important in our firm's ability to succeed are:

1. A comprehensive set of lawn maintenance services – we can do it all

2. A very flexible, menu-oriented system for choosing services

3. An especially well-trained staff, able to deal professionally with customers

4. A very well-organized set of operating procedures that guarantees our dependability

Another major asset is our highly talented and experienced management team. The three key individuals complement each other well, combining backgrounds in diverse group of important areas. Jack Duffy brings expertise in finance and management, Ed Davis brings expertise in lawn maintenance techniques and operations, and Janice Kendall brings expertise in sales and marketing. Together, these strengths cover all of the major aspects of the business with solid experience and a proven record of success.

We are, above all, very customer-focused, committed to solving all of our related customer's needs and doing everything we possibly can to keep them satisfied. This approach will insure that we retain a highly satisfied clientele and get referrals.

(Key person #1)   (...years of experience in... at...)
(Key person #1)   (...years of experience in... at...)

Prototype of proprietary technology

In the initial development phase, we were able to create an operational prototype of (type of prototype). A (patent/copyright) has been applied for and is now pending. This new product offers an important advantage over existing alternatives because...

Aggressive sales force

From the perspective of the customer there is relatively little difference from one product or service to the next. Buyers do not tend to systematically weigh through all the possible options when making a purchasing decision. The ability of the salesperson to get access to the buyer and to persuade the buyer to buy from him or her is a powerful competitive advantage. We (have, will have, are developing) an aggressive sales force that will give us that competitive edge. Important elements in this competitive edge include (our highly experienced sales manager, highly talented salespeople, a careful recruiting plan for sales people, a careful selection process for salespeople, a thorough training program for salespeople, a generous incentive-based compensation structure, a strong sales support program, an ability to generate high quality leads through our marketing efforts).

Ability to develop products that closely match customer's needs

Important to our success (is, will be, has been) our ability to develop new products and services that closely match our customer's needs. By following a systematic process to create our (products or services) we (assure, will assure) that we are meeting our customer's needs better than our competitors. To initiate ideas for new product ideas we first begin with (input from our current customers, input from buyers we know from our past experience, a detailed study of what products or services have been most successful, focus groups of customer's needs, conversations with potential buyers about what they like and dislike about current products or services). Then we develop a (product or service) concept and discuss it with (a focus group, key buyers, our larger customers, potential buyers). We then incorporate their feedback into our final design. [*See Business Plan Example #3*]

Ability to deliver highly personalized service

We are very customer-focused, committed to solving all of our related customer's needs and doing everything we possibly can to keep them satisfied. This approach (has, will, insures) that we retain a highly satisfied clientele, that we get a high rate of repeat business and that we get referrals. Also, especially once we have worked for a customer, we find that the customer is less likely to move to our competition on pricing considerations.

Low cost structure

We have an extremely low cost structure. And just as importantly we are determined to keep our costs low. This allows us to charge low prices, while maintaining our high quality, and still have a good profit margin.

State of the art technology

More so than most of our competitors we are current with the latest technology. We can deliver our customers cutting edge solutions. This gives us an opportunity to develop business with the larger, richer corporations who are willing to pay a substantial premium for the best solutions available today.

Reputation

Over the years we have developed a strong reputation throughout our (market area, industry.) This reputation is based upon... Along with our reputation we have developed a sizable customer base, currently totaling over ... Our reputation has also proved important in our ability to attract new customers.

Financial Situation/Needs

State specifically how much financing you will need, what type of financing, when you will need it, what the financing will be used for, and when you will be able to pay it back. For a start-up business, explain any sources of start-up capital you have already tapped and other sources you plan on using through at least the next year or until operations are underway. You can also here give the reader a quick financial snapshot of your company and refer them to the finance section or financial statements for further information.

Select and edit the statement that best applies....

Basic financial needs statement

At this time we are seeking $... (in equity investment, in a credit line, in an asset-backed loan, in lease financing, in a short term note, in a term loan, etc.) It will be used (to pay down current debt, to finance new products, for working capital, for financing our expansion, to finance receivables, to finance increased inventory, to finance equipment purchases, to begin operations of our business, for seed money, for initial research and development, for marketing, to finance our entry into new markets). We will be able to (pay down the loan

---

Lawn Masters of Newton

Business Plan Example #4

Financial Situation/Needs

At this time we are seeking $30,000 in a credit line, and $180,000 in an asset-backed loan. The credit line will be used for moving expenses, improvements to the new facility, and early season advertising expenditures. The loan will be used to purchase equipment (utility truck and associated tools) for the ten new crews which will be needed to service our expanded customer base. We will be able to pay down the loan completely in 18 months, a process we will begin in August, 1998. The credit line will be cleared before the end of 1998.

in... months, term out the loan over a period of ...months, pay down the credit line for...days once per year, go public within ... years allowing investors to cash out, sell to a larger corporation in about ... years allowing you to cash out your full equity investment).[*See Business Plan Example #4*]

Expansion of existing company

The company has had sales of ($), ($), and ($) over the past three years. We are currently seeking the infusion of ($) in new capital for expansion of the business, which we believe will allow us to grow to the sales of $... within ...years, and profits of $...

Growing company

The company's financial objectives are to reach ($) in sales by (Year), with a gross margin of (%). A loan of ($) is needed to achieve this objective, in the form of a (#)-year note to be paid back by (Month, Year).

Start-up financing

In order to effectively launch the business, we project a total need for ($) in start-up financing. Principal uses of funds are (application of funds), (application of funds), and (application of funds). To date we have raised $... from the three company founders and their relatives. The additional funds we need to raise is $... We project that the company will be profitable by... We project that within ...years of reaching break-even that this new investment could be cashed out by either the founding partners purchasing this investment stake or by replacing the investment stake with bank financing.

Start-up financing in detail

We seek to raise a total of $... in capital to get our business started and finance start-up negative cash flow that we anticipate will last the first ... months of operation. Here is the break-out of the financing we are seeking:

Company founder	$	Equity capital.	100% committed.
Other key managers	$	Equity capital.	100% committed.
Relatives of founder	$	Subordinated debt.	100% committed.
Outside investors	$	Equity capital.	25% committed.
Equipment financing	$	3-10 year leases.	75% committed.
Bank financing	$	Secured credit line	

Bank financing for existing business

This coming year, we project our financial need to peak at $... in the likely scenario. This would be...% (higher, lower) than our peak borrowing during this year and ...% (higher, lower) than our peak borrowing during the ...previous years. Our worst case scenario shows our peak borrowing to be $ As shown in the financial statements the company is currently in a solid financial position. Indicators of our financial strength are (our balance sheet, our income statement, our debt to equity ratio of..., our current ratio of..., etc.)

Financial snapshot of robust business

With sales growth of an average of ...% and net profit growth of an average of ...% over the last ... years, our business is on a roll. We are outpacing our competitors and continuing to improve our market position. Our balance sheet has been strengthening as we increase our retained earnings and decrease our reliance on our credit line. Our current business can easily sustain the current rate of growth without any new financing.

A rapid expansion program

We intend to begin a rapid expansion as outlined in detail in this business plan. In order to accomplish that goal, we will require additional capital. At this point we are seeking $... As shown in our cash flow projections, we anticipate that this will conservatively cover our cash needs for the next ... years.

This page intentionally blank.

VISION STATEMENT

How Do I Get Here?

From the **Main Menu** click on the Business Plan icon. Select Business Plan Text and click OK. You will then be given the option of working on and existing business plan or starting a new one, select the appropriate option and click OK. [If you choose to work on an existing plan the Open dialog box will appear. Click on the plan you want to work on and then click on the Open button.]

The Business Plan window is now visible (see screen shot 1, next page) with your text options in the top half view and your work area below. Click on Vision Statement on the sub-menu bar and the summary text will appear. Double click to select a paragraph from the preformatted text. To edit the text click on the text in the bottom window at the point you wish to edit. All common Windows editing functions are available.

Here is where you describe your vision of what you would like your company to become in the future, such as 5-10 years from now. Try to capture, in relatively few words, the essence of what you envision as the future, major distinctive characteristics of your company. You want to particularly emphasize how your company will be different from other companies in its industry, and how it will be different than the start-up or existing company that it is today.

Select and edit the one statement that best applies

Basic vision statement

Our vision of what our company will become in the future is... Distinctive characteristics of the company will be... The company will differ from it's competitors in that... The company will have developed particularly strong capabilities in ... Our company will be recognized as...

Financial vision statement

Our sales objective is to reach $..... in sales by (date). We plan to achieve a net profit margin of ...% of sales. We intend to reach these objectives largely by (developing new products, opening new markets, increasing sales to current accounts, upgrading our products, increasing market share, a more aggressive sales effort, using a stronger marketing strategy, providing superior service, managing costs closely, cutting overhead, selecting vendors more carefully, maintaining the momentum of our current products, etc.)

Leading participant

Within the next few years, (company name) will grow to become a leading participant in the (industry name) industry, in the (region). We will be known for superior quality (products or services) that will help set the standard in our market.

Personalized service

We want to be thought of as the firm that offers highly personalized service. Our goal is not necessarily to be the largest firm in our market--but instead the firm that really cares about the unique, individual needs of each of its customers.[*See Business Plan Example #5*]

Niche market leader

We intend to be a market leader in the (describe market niche). We want all prospective customers to know that we are the firm that focuses exclusively on this (market niche) and that we also serve it better than any other firm.

Value leader

We intend to be the value leader in our field. We want to be known for very low prices. But we also want to be known for dependable quality at a low price. In one word, we want to be known for "value."

Lawn Masters of Newton

Business Plan Example #5

Vision Statement

Highly personalized service has always been the hallmark of Lawn Masters of Newton. As a very small, owner-operated company, we are able to be very flexible in the way we provide yard maintenance services and do whatever we can to accommodate our customer's needs – from mowing and pruning to fertilizing, mulching and weed control.

Now, we intend to be a stand-out even more as the best managed and most professionally operated firm operating in the City of Newton, Massachusetts. In a field filled with small "mom and pop" operators who run their businesses by the seat of their pants, we intend to distinguish ourselves by planning our services and operations very carefully; having rigorous hiring and training programs; having specific policies and standards for serving customers; and carefully monitoring the quality of our service. We are also going to carefully communicate to our customers the key differences and advantages in doing business with us so our target customers know that choosing us as a supplier is the safe choice for consistent, high quality service. These steps, we believe, will allow Lawn Masters of Newton to double our sales revenue during 1998.

Industry innovator

We want to be seen by our customers as the industry innovator. We particularly want to be known as a company that is trying hard all the time to find new ways of doing business that will benefit its customers.

Most professional

We intend to be a stand-out in our market as the most professionally operated firm. We will be sure that our target customers know that choosing us as a supplier is the safe choice for consistent, high-quality service.[*See Business Plan Example #5*]

Balance between stakeholders

Unlike the shareholder centered companies of old, our vision is to strike a balance between the different important stakeholders in our firm. We see the three pivotal stakeholders as 1) the customers; 2) the employees; 3) the owners. By striving to serve all three equally, we believe that we will also ultimately best serve the interests of each group individually.

Technological leader

We will be seen as on the cutting edge of technology in our industry. When a company wants leading edge solutions--we intend to be the first name to come to mind.

Resolution of current problem/issue

We expect by (date) to have resolved the (describe major current problem or issue facing company). We expect to have overcome this issue by (summarize how you envision overcoming the problem you are now facing). We expect to have become a smoothly functioning organization, with high employee morale, high profitability, growing sales, and we expect to have achieved recognition as a leader in our market.

Milestones

This section is nice feature--but is often not included in business plans and you should not feel compelled to include it either. List a few of the key events or points in time that will be important markers of progress toward the successful achievement of the goals of this business plan. Generally you will want to list between 5 and 10 milestones.

Select and edit one of the following that best applies...

Basic milestone statement

Important milestones (for launching this business, for taking this business to the next level, for this year, for achieving our goals) are...
1. (Milestone)   (Target date)
2. (Milestone)   (Target date)
3. (Milestone)   (Target date)
4. (Milestone)   (Target date)
5. (Milestone)   (Target date)

Milestones for a product business start-up
1. Presentation to investors begins...
2. Financing completed...
3. Product prototype completed...
4. Package design finished...
5. Manufacturing/vendor selection finalized...
6. Sales force in place...

7. Distributors lined up...
8. First product ships...

Milestones for a service business start-up
1. Business plan completed...
2. Financing arranged...
3. Hiring for business opening completed...
4. Advertising/promotion begins...
5. Service begins...

Milestones for an existing business for next year
Important milestones for our business the upcoming year are:
(select the most important milestones and add target dates)
Filling the (new key position)
Shipping the (new product)
Launching an upgrade of (describe product or service)
Launching a new advertising campaign
Adding (describe new sales method) to our sales effort
Beginning the (new service)
Obtaining new financing (describe)

Lawn Masters of Newton

Business Plan Example #6

Milestones

Important milestones for our business the upcoming year are:

Move to new facility	1/15/98
Obtaining financing for new equipment	2/01/98
Launching an upgrade of our services, The Total Lawn Maintenance Package	3/01/98
Launching a new advertising campaign	3/01/98
Adding local cable television advertising to our sales effort	3/01/98
Launching a web site	3/01/98
Achieving sales of $2.2M	9/15/99

Changing vendors for (describe)
Reaching break-even sale volume of $...
Achieving sales of $...
Achieving profitability of...
Entering the (describe new market)
Beginning a new research and development effort for (describe)
Moving to new facilities
Adding an additional facility
Enlarging current facilities
Installing a new computer system
New (describe new equipment) installed
Launching a Web site
New catalog available
Major convention/presentation
Planning process complete
[*See Business Plan Example #6*]

This page intentionally blank.

MARKET ANALYSIS

The Overall Market

Define and describe the overall market that you are competing in. If possible, give the size of the market and cite the source of your information.

How Do I Get Here?

From the **Main Menu** click on the Business Plan icon. Select Business Plan Text and click OK. You will then be given the option of working on and existing business plan or starting a new one, select the appropriate option and click OK. [If you choose to work on an existing plan the Open dialog box will appear. Click on the plan you want to work on and then click on the Open button.]

The Business Plan window is now visible (see screen shot 1, next page) with your text options in the top half view and your work area below.

Click on Market Analysis on the sub-menu bar and the summary text will appear. Double click to select a paragraph from the preformatted text. To edit the text click on the text in the bottom window at the point you wish to edit. All common Windows editing functions are available.

Select and edit the one statement that best applies...

Basic market overview

The overall market for (product or service) in the (world, country, region or town) is approximately $..., according to data from (source of data). The market is growing by about ...% per year. Growth is expected to continue at this pace for the foreseeable future. Sales are relatively steady and not subject to significant cyclical or seasonal variation.

Market overview by distinct product group

The overall size of the industry is currently $... in the (world, country, region, town). Because the industry includes a very diverse group of product types with significantly different characteristics, it is more meaningful to break out analysis of the industry into roughly three (product or service) groups. The first group (specify group) has sales of $... Currently growing at about ...% per year, this group is expected to reach a sales level of $... by the year... The second group (specify group) has sales of $... Currently growing at about ...% per year, this group is expected to reach a sales level of $... by the year ...

The third group (specify group) has sales of $... Currently growing at about ...% per year, this group is expected to reach a sales level of $... by the year ... We intend to compete in the (specify) group and this market analysis will be focused on this group.

Market overview for local service business

We estimate the total current market for (service) at about $... in (town or city). We have derived this number totaling the number of employees providing service at the (number of) current service establishments, then multiplying each employee by our estimate of their average billings per year. The current market for this service appears to be growing because (number) of these firms just opened their doors in the last two years and all of the firms appear to be prospering. Furthermore, as discussed in the customer needs section of this plan, the overall market may be able to grow further if a new business can offer new service dimensions that meet needs not currently being served by existing competitors.[*See Business Plan Example #7*]

Lawn Masters of Newton

Business Plan Example #7

The Overall Market

We estimate the total current market for residential yard maintenance services in Newton, Massachusetts at about $12.5 million. We have derived this number by estimating the percentage of Newton homeowners (20%) who contract for these services and multiplying that number of customers (25,000 occupied housing units * 20% = 5,000) times an average annual fee for mowing, pruning and Spring and Fall clean-up, ($2500).

The current market for this service appears to be growing because several more companies offering these services just opened their doors in the last two years and all of the firms appear to be prospering. Furthermore, as discussed in the customer needs section of this plan, the overall market may be able to grow further if a new business can offer new service dimensions that meet needs not currently being served by existing competitors.

Market overview for local business on per capita basis

The (proposed market area) with (enter amount) population has (enter amount) of (type of business) businesses. This works out to (divide population by businesses) per capita. On the other hand nearby markets with comparable demographics have a much higher number of businesses of this type per capita. Statistics for other markets include (market area 2): (businesses of this type per capita); (market area 3): (businesses of this type per capita); (market area 4): (businesses of this type per capita). These statistics indicate a relatively low level of competition in the proposed market area.

Market overview of stable, mature market

Particularly because this (product or service) has been readily available for many years, the market growth in units has pretty much been in line with the population growth. The market growth in dollar volume, however, has been slightly higher because the typical unit sold is either a higher grade (product or service) or has more features. Similarly future growth, beyond keeping pace with the general population growth, will need to come from selling customers into more expensive products.

Market overview for market about to explode

Potential buyers for this (product or service) number approximately (enter number) in the (world, country, region, city). Basically anyone who meets the following criteria can be considered a potential buyer... Because this product is in its relative infancy and is only being purchased by early adopters, it is difficult to say what percentage of potential buyers will actually purchase the product in the next few years. Estimates of sales potential vary widely from $... to $... In any event, the market is clearly poised for dramatic growth. At this rate, dollar sales are growing at a rate of ...% annually and unit sales are growing at a rate of (enter units) annually. There is no slowdown in sight for growth, and as more and larger competitors enter the marketplace, it is possible that growth will even accelerate in the near future.

Market overview for product/service for corporate market

Once considered a (product or service) for only the largest corporations, now many mid-sized and even smaller firms are buying this (product or service) as well. Because the market for this product is expanding, it is difficult to draw exact boundaries on the size of the potential market, but generally any company over a size of (enter size) is almost certainly using this (product or service) and any company over a size of (enter size) is likely to be at least seriously considering adopting it. We would estimate the total number of companies currently using this (product or service) at (enter amount). The market in dollar size has been estimated at $... and is considered to be growing at the rate of ...%.

Market overview for market on verge of decline

Once a growth area, the market for (product or service) is now flat and is likely to decline in future years as more and more users substitute (alternative product or service). The market is expected to shift gradually, with industry observers projecting a decline of about ...% over the next (years). Beyond this point in time, conversion rate to the (substitute product or service) is difficult to project with estimates varying more widely. In any case this market is not going to disappear overnight and will be a major factor for some time to come. The current sales in this market of $... will dwarf those of the (product service substitute) for some time to come.

Changes in the Market

Summarize important changes and trends in the overall market including any indication you have of what the future holds. Include implications of the changes.

Include and edit all of the following that apply...

Basic trends overview

The most significant development in this marketplace recently has been... Major implications of this trend include... Other important trends include... Implications of these trends are...

Overview for a fast growing local service market

The growth in demand for this service in the local market, as well as in most other markets, outstrips the population growth. Last year growth was estimated to be about ...% nationwide and we have every reason to believe that the local market grew at about the same rate. Beyond population growth, demand for this service is being fueled by the following factors (more people in the target age group, higher disposable incomes, more awareness of the general availability of the service, increased advertising and competition by service providers). Because of the continued presence of these factors, we expect growth in demand for this service to continue at approximately the current rate for the foreseeable future.

Overview for service being provided to corporations

The ongoing trend of corporations to downsize and outsource services such as (specify) has led to very strong growth. Last year growth was estimated at ...% according to (source). Because so much of the growth is coming from companies who have not previously outsourced this service, there is a tremendous potential for new players in this marketplace. New players have the potential to achieve significant sales volumes without having to take customers away from existing competitors. Growth is expected to continue unabated for some time to come.

Lawn Masters of Newton

Business Plan Example #8

Changes in the Market

As the market for yard maintenance services continues to mature, buyers have become increasingly discerning and increasingly aware of and interested in the key feature/benefit differences from one competitor's offering to the next. As a result many, but not all, buyers are placing much added importance on features and performance, and how well the service appears to serve their needs, and are placing less emphasis on price. We believe, for instance, that it will be to our competitive advantage to offer a full range of services – from mowing and pruning to seeding, weeding and insect control – so that customers will not have to contract a variety of different firms to accomplish all of their needs.

Overview of shift in growth from domestic to world markets

While the growth in the domestic market for this (product or service) has been slowing in recent years, overseas markets are showing much more promise. The demographic information (such as rising income levels, higher education levels, and more familiarity with technology) are suggesting that the overseas markets are ripe for dramatically higher growth rates. Although the sales in overseas markets are currently dwarfed by domestic sales, the firms selling overseas are experiencing very fast growth rates and there is every reason to believe that these fast growth rates will continue for years to come, and that eventually the overseas markets may even be larger than the domestic market.

Shift toward more emphasis on features/benefits

As the market for (product or service) continues to mature, buyers have become increasingly discerning and increasingly aware of and interested in the key feature/benefit differences from one competitor's offering to the next. As a result many, but not all, buyers are placing much added importance on features and performance, and how well the (product/service) appears to serve their needs, and are placing less emphasis on price. [*See Business Plan Example #8*]

Shift toward more competition and lower prices

The market is continuing to grow very rapidly in terms of unit sales, increasing approximately ...% during the last year. But the fast growth and increasing size of the market has attracted very tough and determined competitors and the average price per unit has fallen significantly, even as the quality and performance of the typical unit sold has been increasing. As a result while the market continues to grow significantly in dollar sales, increasing approximately ...% during the last year, the dollar volume growth lags significantly behind the growth in unit sales. Also the growth in dollar volume fluctuates more rapidly and is highly susceptible to when major players introduce or find widespread acceptance for the next upgrade of products commanding higher price points.

Shift toward more female buyers

Once overwhelmingly purchased by men, the buying decision for (product or service) is now increasingly being made by women. This trend is being fueled by the changing role of women in society-- including higher income levels, higher levels of professional achievement, and higher education levels. The market for this (product or service) continues to grow among men and they still compose the larger market segment, ...% for the last year for which numbers are available. But the market for women is growing much more rapidly at ...% as opposed to a growth rate of ...% for male buyers. As a result some industry competitors are beginning to either shift the nature of their marketing to be more inclusive of women or are embarking on separate media campaigns specifically aimed at women.

Shift toward younger buyers

Just several years ago the market for this (product or service) was predominantly people over the age of (specify age), with over ...% of sales to this age group in the year .... But in the last year, sales to the over (specify age) had fallen to ...%. The biggest growth is taking place in the (specify age) group which now comprises over ...% of total market sales. This shift is apparently being caused by higher disposable income and more sophisticated tastes among younger people. As a result some industry competitors are beginning to position some or all of their (products or services) toward the younger generation.

Shift toward smaller companies

While once only larger and mid-size companies were considered viable prospects for this (product or service), now smaller companies are increasingly purchasing it. Companies with sales of as little as $... or as few as (number) of employees are now expanding the use of this (product or service). Part of this trend is being fueled by lower costs and wider availability as well as an increased tendency to view the (product or service) as an integral part of any forward-looking company's business operation, not just a "nice to have" option.

Shift to home-based businesses

Beyond the overall growth in the market of potential small business users, there is another very important trend shaping the market. This is the growth of home-based businesses. More and more people are running businesses out of their homes and many of the people running these businesses are sophisticated individuals who often previously worked at larger corporations. Running a home-based business has increasingly lost the negative stigma that once accompanied it, and especially with recent advances in technology, has become a very viable option for many people. Home-based businesses often have different needs from their office-based counterparts. They also frequently have a different attitude to business that has important implications for positioning, marketing strategy and advertising.

Market segments

Carefully defining market segments is crucial for establishing or reviewing your business strategy, your product positioning, and your marketing strategy. Different markets tend to be segmented in different ways. Carefully consider the most meaningful way your market is segmented--especially considering the viewpoint of potential buyers. For example, is the market segmented by price point? By different product/service functions? By features? By target consumer groups? By geography? By specialty? By sales channel? By delivery method? Also bear in mind that many markets are segmented in more than one way.

Include and edit all of the following that apply...

Basic segmentation statement

The market is primarily segmented by (price point, product function, features, target consumer groups, geography, specialty, sales channel, delivery method, or ...). The number one segment in size is defined as .... It comprises approximately ...% of the total market. And it is growing (faster, slower or about the same) as the total market at the pace of about ...% per year. The number two segment in size is defined as .... It comprises approximately ...% of the total market. And it is growing (faster, slower or about the same) as the total market at the pace of about ...% per year. The number three segment in size is defined as .... It comprises approximately ...% of the total market. And it is growing (faster, slower or about the same) as the total market at the pace of about ...% per year. The number four segment in size is defined as .... It comprises approximately ...% of the total market. And it is growing (faster, slower or about the same) as the total market at the pace of about ...% per year.

Quick approach to segmentation

The basic market segments are:
1. (Describe segment) (enter percent)% of total market.

2. (Describe segment) (enter percent)% of total market.
3. (Describe segment) (enter percent)% of total market.
4. (Describe segment) (enter percent)% of total market.

No segmentation

While there are obvious differences including features, pricing and other attributes from one firm's (product or service) to the next, the market has not become segmented. Each competitor is more or less competing for the same customer and each (product or service) is overwhelmingly aimed at accomplishing the same function without significant competitive differentiation. While firms go to great length to tout their competitive differences, they still are basically competing within the same marketplace for the same customers.

Increasing segmentation

Until recently, buyers were thought to have relatively similar needs, and while there was some differences from one (product or service) to the next, there were not clearly defined segments and all industry participants more or less competed with one another head on. But recently this has begun to change with market segmentation emerging--although it is much more obvious in some potential markets than others. The most clearly segmented parts of the market are.... In these segments, buyers are responding well to product or service) offerings aimed at specific needs. However buyers are not responding as well to attempted segmentation in other parts of the market such as attempts to segment the market by....

Professional/consumer/institutional segments

The market is divided by its three distinct user groups: professional--businesses buying the (product or service) for business use; consumer--individual consumers buying the (product or service) for personal use; and institutional--schools and government agencies buying the (product or service) for use at their facilities. The professional segment is estimated to be ...% of the market; the consumer segment ...% of the market; and the institutional segment ...% of the market. The basic products being sold into each market are quite similar or in many cases identical. However there are substantial differences in customer needs and concerns and the selling and marketing strategies used by competitors are quite a bit different from one market to the next.

Luxury/standard/economy segments

The market can be broken into basically three segments: the (luxury or high performance) segment for consumers that are more interested in higher quality or the most features and are less concerned with price; (the standard or mid-range) segment for consumers who want to strike a balance between quality, features and price; and the (economy or basic) segment for consumers who are most concerned with price. While some (products or services) are on the borderline between these groupings, this segmentation applies to most offerings and most potential consumers are generally likely to only consider options within one segment at any one time.[*See Business Plan Example #9*]

Lawn Masters of Newton

Business Plan Example #9

Market segments

The market can be broken into basically three segments: the full-service segment for consumers who are more interested in a comprehensive approach and are less concerned with price; the mid-range segment for consumers who want more than a bare bones package; and the economy segment for consumers who are most concerned with price. While some yard maintenance companies are on the borderline between these groupings, this segmentation applies to most service offerings, and most potential consumers are generally likely to only consider options within one segment at any one time.

Secondary segmentations

In addition to the major segmentation of the market, (some, all, one) segment is also segmented by (price point, product function, features, target consumer groups, geography, specialty, sales channel, delivery method, or ...). The size and growth of the sub segments that are most relevant for us are as follows. The (sub segment #1) is approximately $... and growing at approximately ...% per year. The (sub segment #2) is approximately $... and growing at approximately ...% per year.

Target market and customers

Define and describe the target market segment or customers that you are primarily going to focus on in your business. Unless you have a clear idea of your target market, you may not want to complete this section until after you have completed the strategy section.

Include and edit all of the following that apply...

Basic consumer target market statement

Our target market is... Our target market is defined by consumers that (describe target consumers). Common characteristics of (products or services) serving this market are....
We are well-suited to serve this market because....

Basic business target market statement

Our target market is... Our target market is defined by companies (with sales between $... and $...) in (industries) in the (city, metro area, region, nation). Other common characteristics that define our core market are... We are well-suited to serve this market because....

Multiple tiered targets

Our primary target market segment will be...... We feel that this market will be easier to enter and also holds more long-term promise because of its high growth rate. We will also give secondary emphasis to the following markets... Because the (products or services) used by these different market segments are highly similar, we believe we can effectively cover all of these different segments without spreading our efforts too thin, however, we will give our major marketing effort to our primary target market.

Multiple markets, equal focus

We will focus on (two, three, four, etc.) target markets...(describe each market). Each of these markets shows good promise and can be well served by the same business because of their highly similar (product or service) needs.

Niche market focus

We intend to focus very narrowly on one particular market niche: (describe niche). Buyers and potential buyers with these needs are not being specifically targeted or particularly well served by other companies. While this market niche is small enough not to attract a lot of attention from the national corporations, it is large enough for us to realize our growth expectations for the next 5-10 years. It is also a niche that we believe our company will be uniquely well-qualified to address because of....

Local service business

We intend to direct all our efforts to within the town of (name town). To reach our sales goals over the next five years we estimate that we will need to achieve about ... percent market share--not enough to be likely to initiate an aggressive competitive response to our market entry. While we could easily travel to surrounding towns to provide service, we feel that from a marketing standpoint we are much better off focusing on one town. We can build sales momentum more easily by focusing on one town--for example we can buy larger ads in one local newspaper and we can more quickly build a word-of-mouth reputation. The demographics in this town, especially...., appear particularly good for our business.[*See Business Plan Example #10*]

Focus on specific companies

Our business will narrowly focus on just a handful of companies that our firm, or key employees at our firm, have had a prior relationship with. These companies are.... Our relationships and past experiences with these companies makes us uniquely well suited to serve their needs and gives us a strong competitive advantage. By limiting our focus to these very few firms, we can insure that we will remain extremely responsive to their needs and be able to offer unparalleled service.

Customer characteristics

Analyzing customer characteristics helps you position and refine your products and services and develop your marketing strategy. Include characteristics that are more common among your target buyers than in the general population, but don't limit yourself to characteristics that are necessarily shared by all or even most buyers.

Lawn Masters of Newton

Business Plan Example #10

Target market and customers

We intend to direct all of our effort within the City of Newton, Massachusetts. To reach our sales goals, we estimate that we will need to achieve about 20% market share -- not enough to provoke an aggressive competitive response.

While we could easily travel to surrounding towns to provide yard maintenance services, we feel that from a marketing standpoint we are much better off focusing on Newton. One advantage is that we will be able to build sales momentum more easily by purchasing larger ads in one local newspaper. We feel that we will also be able to more quickly build a word-of-mouth reputation. The demographics of Newton, of course, are particularly good for our business.

Include and edit all of the following that apply...

Basic target consumer characteristics statement

Our target consumers tend to be (male, female), aged (enter range), (single, married, married with children, etc.), (education level), with a household income of (enter income), (works full-time, part-time, is a student, is a homemaker, is retired), typical occupations include (enter occupations), they live in (cities, suburbs, towns, specific neighborhoods, etc.). They tend to read (list types of or specific magazines and newspapers), they tend to listen to (list types of or specific radio stations), they tend to watch (list types of or specific TV shows), and they tend to access the Internet (often, occasionally, seldom). They often belong to the following community organizations... They often participate in the following non-business activities... Other pertinent characteristics include...

Basic target company characteristic statement

Our target companies tend to have sales between $... and $..., they tend to have between ... and ... employees, they tend to be in the following industry(ies), ... , and they tend to be located in ... These companies tend to be (start-ups, relatively new firms, established firms), (fast growing, growing, stable, experiencing stiffening competition), and (privately-held or publicly held). Other pertinent characteristics include...

Basic buyer at target company characteristics statement

The key decision-maker at the companies we are targeting tend to hold the position of (enter position) and usually report to (enter supervisor). They tend to be (male, female), aged (enter range), (single, married, married with children, etc.), (education level), with a household income of (enter income), they live in (cities, suburbs, towns, specific neighborhoods, etc.). They tend to read the following trade publications (enter specific publications), the following business publications (list types of or specific magazines and newspapers), and the following consumer publications (list types of or specific magazines and newspapers). They tend to listen to (list types of or specific radio stations), they tend to watch (list types of or specific TV shows or enter little or no TV), and they tend to access the Internet (often, occasionally, seldom). They often belong to the following industry and business organizations... They frequently attend the following trade shows, conferences, seminars, and charity events... They tend to participate in the following activities outside of the workplace...

Additional company business buyer characteristics

Our target buyers make approximately (enter amount) of purchasing decisions per month. They tend to meet with approximately (enter number) of salespeople per month. Common preferred methods of communication are (in-person visits, phone, e-mail, fax, or letters). They usually (answer or don't answer) their own phone. (Or their phone is usually answered by an assistant or is on voice mail.)   They control or influence budgets in the range of (give range). Expenditures for (products or services) like ours consume approximately ...% of their budget. Our (product or service) category is a (must-have purchase item, an important purchase item, a highly desirable purchase item, a clearly useful but not important purchase item, a marginal purchase item).

Tiered evaluation of customer characteristics

All of our prospective customers share the need for.... Almost all of our customers have the following characteristics... Many, but not all, of our customers have these characteristics as well... In addition some, but less than a majority of our customers have these characteristics... [*See Business Plan Example #11*]

Customer characteristic groups of particular interest

Of particular interest are the customers with ... characteristics because they compose a highly identifiable group with specific needs, yet they are not being well served by any current product or service offering.

Lawn Masters of Newton

Business Plan Example #11

Customer characteristics

All of our prospective customers share the need for professional yard maintenance services. Most of them have the following characteristics: Two-income homeowners; own at least quarter-acre lots with lawns, shrubs and trees; college educated; concerned with the environment and the proper use of pesticides and other chemical treatments. Many, but not all, of our target customers are middle-aged or elderly.

Customer needs

Be highly specific about the benefits the purchaser derives from the product/service and the needs that it fulfills. Include direct and indirect, tangible and intangible benefits. For example by buying a new sofa a buyer gets not only a place to sit, but also improves the decor of the house, impresses friends, and enjoys seeing it in the living room.

Basic customer needs statement

The most obvious needs this (product or service) addresses is the following... Additional needs that it meets are...

Identifying an unfilled need

The basic need of target customers is... Virtually all competing (products or services) address this basic need fairly well. Other needs that are relatively important include...The various (products or services) currently available address these needs by .... Some customers have a need for... This need is not being well met by existing alternatives. Furthermore for some buyers it is an important enough need that they would buy a new product largely on the basis of how well it filled this need.

Increasingly demanding buyers

The basic need that buyers are looking for is... But because of the many competitive alternatives, buyers are demanding that other needs be satisfied as well. Common demands from buyers now include.... In addition some buyers are beginning not only to request, but to insist upon...

Variable needs

Even within the market segment that we are targeting, customer needs vary significantly from one buyer to the next. Companies are currently dealing with this broad range of wants

---

Lawn Masters of Newton

Business Plan Example #12

Customer needs

Even within the market segment that we are targeting, customer needs vary significantly from one buyer to the next. Most companies are currently dealing with this broad range of market demands by specializing in servicing a narrow portion of the market segment; i.e., just offering lawn mowing, or focusing exclusively on re-seeding and fertilizing services. We intend to take a "menu" approach, in which customers can pick and choose any level of services they need.

by (offering a highly customized approach, offering a broad range of product or service options, specializing in servicing a narrow portion of the market segment, offering add-on features or services).[*See Business Plan Example #12*]

Changing needs

Historically buyers in this market have been overwhelmingly concerned with the following need... Recently however, because of the following changes in the marketplace...., many buyers have become increasingly concerned about .... This need is not being adequately addressed by current solutions that are available. But our company intends to directly address this need and use it as leverage to quickly build market share.

Customer buying decisions

Describe the steps and the thought process that buyers go through in making purchasing decisions. Include rational as well as emotional elements of their decision-making process and identify all participants typically involved in making or influencing the decision.

Basic customer buying decision statement

These are the typical steps that buyers will typically go through in considering purchasing the (product or service)... The single most important factor in determining a buyer's decision is... Other important factors are...

The impulse purchase

The buying decision is an impulse purchase made instantly on-the-spot. Hence key purchasing factors include availability of product, prominence of display, any special display fixtures, signage, packaging, and a low impulse price point.

Planned purchase

The buying decision is made in advance of the actual purchase time. The buyer makes a conscious decision to purchase the product or service. Importantly, the buyer either (does or does not) decide in advance of visiting or calling the purchasing establishment what specific brand or model or type to purchase. Because this is a planned purchase, display and ready, easy availability of the (product or service) are less important factors. Absolute low price also tends to be less crucial. What is most important is reaching and influencing the potential buyer before the purchase decision is made.

Presentation purchase

The buying decision is almost always made (at an in-person or during a telephone) sales presentation. The personal touch appears to be essential for moving buyers to action for this (product or service) because.... To support the sales presentation (advertising, product recognition, incentives) (are very important, somewhat important, are of uncertain importance, are not important) in closing the sale.[*See Business Plan Example #13*]

Buying the company

Buyers in this market tend to put much weight on the company rather than just on the particular merits of the product or service being offered. While this tends to favor more established companies, it can work to the advantage of a newer company that carefully hones a very specific and favorable image for itself. [*See Business Plan Example #13*]

Rational/emotional decision

Buyers tend (or don't) tend to make a careful decision based primarily upon an examination of the (product or service) merits. Instead emotional factors come into play including...

Competitive comparisons

Buyers tend to (very carefully, somewhat carefully, very casually, not at all) examine (product or service) features and benefits before making a purchasing decision.

The herd mentality

The buyer's perspective of the (product's or services) relative success or lack of success for other buyers plays an important role in the decision-making process. Buyers in this market feel very nervous about adopting a (product or service) that they do not feel has been widely adopted. At the same time, they are more likely to buy a product just because others have already purchased the product. For many buyers their feeling about the (product's or service') relative acceptance and success plays a more important role in their decision to buy it than their own careful examination of its actual merits.

Special closing incentives

Buyers are increasingly expecting to get a "special incentive" to make the final buying decision. And the more special incentives are offered, the more buyers seem to expect them. Special incentives that buyers seem to respond best to include...

Corporate buying decisions

Corporate buyers of our product seem to respond best to the following sales pattern: first, having a chance to read printed literature; second, being called to action by a phone call; third, being shown the specifics of the product or service during a personal presentation; fourth, being carefully followed up with over a period of several (days, weeks) as the decision to purchase is considered and often discussed with other people.

Multiple decision-makers at corporations

The (president, buyer, sales manager, controller, purchasing agent) is usually the primary decision maker, and crucial for moving the decision ahead. However other people, such as ... are often able to influence the decision-making process or veto the decision to buy.

Couples making decisions...

When we sell to married couples both the husband and the wife play a role in the decision-making. Usually the (husband or wife) plays the key decision-making role, but the other spouse must at least acquiesce for the purchase decision to move ahead. Nonetheless, we have found it is highly desirable to be able to make the sales presentation when both spouses are home. [*See Business Plan Example #13*]

Buying display space...

While in this industry, retailers do not technically require slotting fees, they seldom will buy a product without a heavy commitment to buy co-op advertising--of which the manufacturer must pay 100%. Co-op launch funds can be as high as $... for a single product at a major account.

Lawn Masters of Newton

Business Plan Example #13

Customer buying decisions

The buying decision is almost always made at an in-person sales presentation. The personal touch appears to be essential for moving buyers to action for yard maintenance services because homeowners in Newton feel very protective and proprietary about their property. To support the sales presentation pricing incentives are not very important in closing the sale – but testimonials, especially from nearby neighbors, are.

Buyers in this market tend to put a lot of weight on the company rather than just on the particular merits of the product or service being offered. We intend to make this work to our advantage by carefully developing a very specific and favorable image for ourselves.

When we sell to married couples both the husband and the wife play a role in the decision making. Usually the husband plays the key decision-making role, but the other spouse must at least acquiesce for the purchase decision to move ahead. For this reason, we have found that it is highly desirable to be able to make the sales presentation when both spouses are home.

This page intentionally blank.

COMPETITIVE ANALYSIS

How Do I Get Here?

From the **Main Menu** click on the Business Plan icon. Select Business Plan Text and click OK. You will then be given the option of working on and existing business plan or starting a new one, select the appropriate option and click OK. [If you choose to work on an existing plan the Open dialog box will appear. Click on the plan you want to work on and then click on the Open button.]

The Business Plan window is now visible (see screen shot 1, next page) with your text options in the top half view and your work area below.

Click on Competitive Analysis on the sub-menu bar and the summary text will appear. Double click to select a paragraph from the preformatted text. To edit the text click on the text in the bottom window at the point you wish to edit. All common Windows editing functions are available.

Industry Overview

Present a concise overall picture of the industry. Useful information may include industry structure, degree of competitiveness, level of profitability, and other important characteristics.

Include and edit all of the following that apply...

Basic industry overview statement

Total sales in this industry nationwide are $... Companies in this industry range in size from $.... in sales to $... in sales. The industry is (dominated by one company..., dominated by a few large players, primarily composed of mid-sized firms ranging in size from $... to $..., composed largely of smaller firms under $... who account for the vast majority of sales). Companies compete with one another generally (across the globe, across the nation, within particular regions such as..., within particular metropolitan areas, locally, within a particular city or town). Companies within this industry are best categorized by (their size, the market segment they serve, the type of customer they serve, by their sales method, their production method, their types of product, their types of services, their specialization, their relative pricing/quality). Hence the industry can be divided into the following categories:
1. (Category or segment 1) (size of segment 1)
2. (Category or segment 2) (size of segment 2)
3. (Category or segment 3) (size of segment 3)

Important characteristics of each category are...

Number and size of competitors

Across the country there are ...companies in this industry. In the market that we will be competing, (describe market segment or geographical location), there are ... companies. The range in size from... to... However most firms are in the ...size range. Some of the firms focus exclusively on this type of (product or service), while for others it is just one part of their business.

Companies grouped by category

There are several different kinds of competitors in this industry. The major determining difference in this industry is (sales method, production method, marketing method, target segment, size of company, specialization, etc.). Companies that are similar in this regard generally tend to compete much more directly and compete in more similar ways than companies that are not similar in this regard.

Industry segments

This industry can be broken into the following segments:
1. (Describe segment 1) (size or number of companies)
2. (Describe segment 2) (size or number of companies)
3. (Describe segment 3) (size or number of companies)
 (Segment 1) is characterized by... (Segment 2) is characterized by... (Segment 3) is characterized by...

Description of industry participants

The (name) industry can be thought of as firms that offer the following (list common types of products or services). In addition some firms in this industry also offer (list less common types of products or services). Most firms are (owner operated, professionally managed, publicly held, subsidiaries or divisions of larger corporations). Most firms have been in business (for many years, for at least ten years, for just a few years). The most common sales and marketing methods that companies use are... Customers tend to (be highly loyal to one company, switch companies often, be open-minded to trying new companies, stay with one product or service).

Common consumer service industry structure

Competition is highly limited by locality. Customers are reluctant to use service providers based in distant locations and even tend to do business with a service business that specifically focuses on their (city, town, region, metro area). As a result, in our target market (specify), there are only (enter number) direct competitors. Because these companies are private, exact sales information is not available, but based on their number of (employees, service trucks, etc.) I would estimate that no one competitor dominates, and that the market share of each firm ranges between ...% and ...%. [*See Business Plan Example #14*]

Common business service industry structure

Competitors tend to focus on (specific cities or regions, industries, functions, sizes of companies, etc.)   Because of the tendency to specialize, the degree of competition varies widely from one selling situation to the next. Competition tends to be most intense for larger volume accounts... And competition tends to be less intense for potentially smaller volume accounts...

Hyper-competitive

The industry can be best characterized as hyper-competitive. There are many firms competing more or less directly for the same customers. Competing companies (products or services) are highly similar, yet, without a clear difference from one to the next. Profit margins tend to be relatively thin and market shares within the industry tend to fluctuate from one year to the next.

Mild competition

Competition in this industry is rather mild. There are only a few direct competitors.

Lawn Masters of Newton

Business Plan Example #14

Industry Overview

Competition in the yard maintenance field is highly limited by locality. Customers are reluctant to use service providers based in distant locations and even tend to do business with a service organization that specifically focuses on their city or town. As a result, in our target market of Newton, Massachusetts, there are only eight significant direct competitors. Because these companies are private, exact sales information is not available, but based on their number of employees, we estimate that no one competitor dominates, and that the market share for each firm ranges between 10% and 15%.

The actual competition in this industry is rather mild. Customers do not to switch firms very often and do not tend to carefully comparison shop before making buying decisions. Market shares have tended to be relatively stable. Competitors do not make aggressive marketing moves, such running predatory or comparative advertising campaigns. There is little competition on price, and price incentives or promotions are rare. Relationships are of primary importance. Customers tend not to seriously consider unsolicited overtures from new vendors, and it takes a strong reason for them to specifically request a presentation from a new vendor.

The industry obviously has pronounced seasonal swings. The first quarter tends to account for less than 10% of sales. The second and third quarters represent the vast majority, over 80%, of sales. Some Fall clean-up work extends into the fourth quarter, bringing in, like the first quarter, about 10% of the annual revenue. Seasonality in this industry has important implications – because the billings have to take place during the Spring and Summer months, it is essential to carry out any sales or marketing activities during the late Winter, so that customers can be signed up and ready by late March or early April.

Ease of entry in this industry can be characterized as moderately difficult. Barriers do not involve capital requirements or staffing issues, but rather the difficulty of developing a customer base from scratch.

Most firms in this industry are sole proprietorships, or closely-held corporations. These ownership patterns have been relatively steady for years. Debt loads in the industry tend to be relatively marginal, in the range of 20% of total capitalization.

Customers do not switch firms very often and do not tend to carefully comparison shop before making buying decisions. Market shares tend to be relatively stable. Competitors do not make aggressive marketing moves such as running predatory or comparative advertising campaigns. There is little competition on price, and price incentives or promotions are rare. [*See Business Plan Example #14*]

Business is transaction oriented

On-going relationships are not important in this industry. This doesn't mean that relationships don't matter at all, but instead, customers tend to put more weight on their perception of the supplier's ability to meet their needs today, as opposed to whether or not they previously did business with the company. As a result there is relatively little customer loyalty in this industry. Multiple competitors tend to either serve the same customers simultaneously, or they tend to find that their customers are often switching from one firm to the next.

Relationships are important

Customers do not switch suppliers often and tend to be relatively satisfied with current vendors. The strength of the relationship between customer and seller plays just as important a role as any other factor such as features, pricing, etc. Customers tend not to seriously consider unsolicited overtures from new vendors, and it takes a strong reason for them to specifically request a presentation from a new vendor.

Industry dominated by few key players

While there are many different firms competing in this industry, competition is dominated by (one, two, three, etc.) firms. Together these firms have a market share of ...%. These firms are by far the most visible in the industry and their moves tend to determine industry direction and the nature of the competition. The larger firms tend to have much broader (product or service) lines, while the smaller firms tend to be more specialized.

Structure in our target market

The general market that we are serving (specify) is of course a huge and complex industry about which there are large amounts of information available from many sources. But because we are specifically targeting a very limited part of this market, we will limit the discussion to this market segment. The (specify segment) is characterized by (level of competition). It (is or is not) dominated by (one, two, three, etc.) firms. The type of firms that we are going to compete most directly with are characterized by...

The power is held by...

In this industry, power is really held by the (manufacturers, wholesalers, retailers, customers, end-users, suppliers, etc.) They tend to be much larger firms and each of them wields considerable power by controlling access to .... On the other hand, the firms that they (buy from, sell to, etc.) tend to be much smaller and hence lack market power. The concentration of this power has considerable impact on the industry. For example...

Cyclical

This industry tends to be highly cyclical. Sales generally fall and rise in parallel to the basic (national, world, or specific industry) economic cycles. At the low point of the cycle not only sales, but also prices, and of course, profits, fall significantly. At the high point of the cycle sales rise, prices rise, profits soar, and capacity is strained until the industry invests in more plants and equipment.

Seasonality

The industry has consistent seasonal swings. First quarter tends to be ...% of sales; second quarter tends to be ...% of sales; third quarter ...% of sales; fourth quarter ...% of sales. Industry profits are overwhelmingly concentrated in the ... quarter. Seasonality in this industry has the following important implications... [*See Business Plan Example #14*]

Financial outlook

The profit levels in this industry are (high, low, mixed, in the range of ...% of sales). Profits are (fairly consistent from one firm to the next, highly inconsistent from one firm to the next, overwhelmingly concentrated at the larger firms). Firms that have higher profit margins tend to share the following characteristics... Firms in this industry tend to be (cash rich, have excellent access to capital, have moderate debt, have high levels of debt).

A tough, but growing industry

While the rapid growth of this industry has attracted many new firms from start-ups to large established corporations, many firms have experienced huge losses. Some have withdrawn from the field, others continue to struggle along, others have been acquired by more successful firms, and still others have fallen into bankruptcy or even liquidation. Problems that have created the most problems for companies in this industry include...

A highly lucrative industry

Historically this industry has been highly lucrative with high margins, below average competition, steadily rising sales, and solid financial performances. What has limited entrance to this industry is (the need for specialized training, most people do not want to operate a business of this type, significant investment requirements, the difficulty of getting customers to switch from existing companies, how well-entrenched existing firms are).

Ease of entry

Ease of entry in this industry can be characterized as (describe). Many firms (successfully or unsuccessfully try to) enter this field each year. Firms that have been most successfully entering this field have tended to... Firms that have not been successful trying to enter this field have tended to... [*See Business Plan Example #14*]

Ownership

Most firms in this industry are (sole proprietorships, partnerships, closely-held corporations, publicly held corporations, subsidiaries of publicity held corporations.) Ownership patterns have been (relatively steady, shifting toward more ownership by publicly held corporations). Debt loads in the industry tend to be (relatively marginal, low, average, moderately high, high, in the range of ...% of total capitalization). [*See Business Plan Example #14*]

Nature of competition

Here the key is finding the one or very few ways that companies focus most of their competitive effort--not just listing every way in which companies compete. What does top management focus on? What does ad copy focus on? What do companies spend a lot of time or money on? What do companies emphasize in sales pitches or on their packaging? What do they focus on when they compare their products to their competitors?

Include just the very most important that apply...

Basic competition statement

Competition in this industry focuses largely on (price, quality, features, performance, specialization, expertise, reliability, technology, customer relationships, marketing, advertising, sales, publicity, distribution, serving particular market niches, appealing to particular consumers). This is emphasized in advertising, in press releases, and in sales pitches. While companies compete on other dimensions as well, this is the primary direction that most competitive effort goes into. Apparently the management at most companies feel that this factor is most important in consumer buying decisions. Important secondary focuses of competition are... [*See Business Plan Example #15*]

Features are king...

Competitive effort largely focuses on features. New features are regularly added and are very highly trumpeted in press releases, in advertising, and in sale pitches.

Quality counts...

Quality is a major focus on the competitive battle in this industry. Quality is usually meant to mean... Quality is conveyed to potential buyers by... Price is seldom a competitive factor, and firms that do, compete on price risk undermining their quality image.

Price is the bottom line...

Most competitors focus overwhelmingly on price. Price is emphasized again and again in advertising and even included in some store's taglines. As a result, companies work very hard to drive their costs down. They try to squeeze the last penny out of vendors. And they work hard to cut their overhead and other costs of doing business.

Customer focused

Competition in this industry is customer-focused. Companies go out of their way to respond very quickly to serving the unique requests and desires of individual customers. They remain flexible and adaptive to their customers needs and usually create a strong amount of loyalty with customers that they serve.

Lawn Masters of Newton

Business Plan Example #15

Nature of competition

Competition focuses on the quality of service, particularly on reliability. Price is seldom emphasized and tends not to vary much between most firms. Instead firms try to emphasize to their customers how their service is better than that of their competitors. For example they might mention in their advertising or sales pitches the number of years in service in Newton and the guaranteed availability of crews and equipment.

Companies strive not only to build relationships with their current customers, but also to emphasize to new customers how strong and beneficial a long-term relationship with them will be. The emphasis is on selling not a particular product or service, but the whole company. Often extra intangibles, such as direct knowledge of an established customer's specific landscaping situation, are emphasized to show that the value of the whole relationship is greater than the sum of the actual services that are being sold.

Quality of service...
Competition focuses on the quality of service. Price is seldom emphasized and tends not to vary much between most firms. Instead firms try to emphasize to their customers how their service is better than that of their competitors. For example, they might mention in their advertising or sales pitch (number of years in service, levels of training, licenses, certificates, size of company, availability, quality of parts, guarantees, etc.)

Sales-driven
While there is some differences between the competing (products or services), the heart of competition is the sales process. Usually, the more effective salesperson will get the sale. As a result, companies spend a huge amount of their senior management time focused on improving their sales process and a high percentage of their budgets on sales costs. Companies are particularly cautious about losing salespeople to competing firms and quick to hire talented salespeople with industry experience.

Product-driven
This industry is product driven. New products are introduced at the rate of ... New products tend to account for about ...% of total sales. The life cycle of products is typically short, such as.... A very large percentage of new products ...% quickly fail and are withdrawn from the market.

Product upgrades
Products tend to be upgraded on average approximately every ... (months/years). Major products tend to be upgraded more frequently, such as every ... (months/years). Product

upgrades (usually, often, usually not, seldom) represent substantial changes. They are (usually, often, usually not, seldom) accompanied by much marketing attention.

Positioning

The competitive battle in this market is waged in the mind of potential consumers. Most buyers are pre-sold on one brand of product or another before they actually buy it. As a result, advertising and other kinds of marketing are particularly important.

Spoils to the winner

People tend to buy (products and services) in this industry just because they are the market leader. This makes competing difficult for small companies--except for those firms with very specialized products or services. As a result, firms spend huge amounts of money and effort when they feel they have a chance of taking over the leadership position for any key (product or service).

Trade emphasis

Competition focuses primarily on selling to retailers or wholesalers, because the task of selling to end consumers is seen as largely outside the control of the manufacturer. This is particularly true because products in this industry are low priced impulse products.

Relationship-driven

Companies strive not only to build relationships with their current customers, but also to emphasize to new customers how strong and beneficial a long-term relationship with them will be. The emphasis is on selling not a particular product or service, but the whole company. Often extra intangibles such as.... are emphasized to show that the value of the whole relationship is greater than the sum of the actual (products or services) that are being sold. [*See Business Plan Example #15*]

Local proximity

In this industry local proximity is a major competitive factor. Firms not only emphasize that they are conveniently located, but they go beyond this to infer that there is extra goodwill that accompanies their ties to the local community. Advertising statements such as (local ownership, based in ...., a local business, etc.) show how much importance is placed on closeness to the community.

Technology driven

Competition in this industry focuses on technology. Firms invest great of effort in striving for technical advances over their competition. Marketing tends to emphasize technical differences.

Promotionally driven

The nature of competition is becoming increasingly promotionally driven. More than half of all sales are closed with some kind of special offer. The most common promotional offer is the ... Other promotional offers include ...

Mixed nature of competition

Different companies focus their competitive energies in many different ways in this industry. Some firms, for example, give their primary competitive focus to... Examples of these firms are... Other firms give their competitive focus to... Examples of these firms are... And still other firms give their competitive focus to...

Changes in the Industry

Summarize major pertinent changes that are shaping the industry. Describe what the impact of these changes are on the different players in the industry including, if applicable, suppliers, your competitors, dealers, wholesalers, retailers, and consumers..

Include and edit all of the following that apply...

Basic industry changes statement

Current changes taking place in this industry are (consolidation, the entrance of major corporations, the entrance of many new firms, the exit of several important participants, the closing of many smaller firms, a trend toward specialization, a shift in power to..., an increased reliance on outsourcing for..., the bundling of..., a shift toward one-stop-shopping, the emerging threat of a product substitute, an increase in costs, a shift toward more price competition). As a result, within a few years the industry will be.... Implications of these changes include...

Growth

The industry is currently experiencing a period of (rapid growth, moderate growth, average growth, flat sales, declining sales, uncertainty, volatility) caused by... In the years ahead this trend is expected to (accelerate, continue, abate, slow down) because of... The current (growth, stability, decline) in the industry has had the following implications... [*See Business Plan Example #16*]

Consolidation

The industry is going through a period of consolidation as (larger firms are acquiring smaller firms, larger firms are expanding and smaller firms are going out of business, a few dominant players are increasing their control of the industry). This consolidation has had the following implications...

Major corporations entering the industry

The fast growth of this marketplace has attracted major corporate players, several of whom have already launched products, and several of whom are expected to do so shortly. They are launching their products with major advertising and promotional expenditures and using the clout of their national sales forces to roll out their products. As a result, it is becoming a much more difficult climate for smaller players, especially less established ones, to launch products that are not specialized or aimed at narrow market segments.

Lawn Masters of Newton

Business Plan Example #16

Changes in the Industry

The industry in currently experiencing a period of moderate growth caused by the aging of the population base, the increasing value of residential property in Newton, and the robust economy. In the years ahead, this trend is expected to continue. We believe that there will be more and more customers, and that they will be looking for one single source for their yard maintenance needs. This gives a huge advantage to firms that offer an extremely flexible and broad array of services, and a disadvantage to those that don't.

Shift to fewer vendors

To improve their operating efficiencies, customers have been cutting their lists of vendors and consolidating their purchasing to a few larger suppliers and wholesalers. They have also become increasingly demanding of their suppliers, for example insisting that all vendors use Electronic Data Interchange, requiring their suppliers to always be in stock of critical items, and enforcing strict shipping requirements.

Power shift

Power in this industry is shifting to the (manufacturers, wholesalers, retailers, customers, end-users, suppliers, etc.) They are growing in size and clout and have the ability to become increasingly demanding of the companies with which they deal. Implications of this trend are...

Outsourcing

Industry participants are outsourcing more and more of their work. Functions that are most likely to be outsourced include... Possible impact of this change is...

Strategic alliances

As this industry continues to grow and become increasingly complex, companies are forming strategic alliances. Common strategic alliances are between firms that (describe relationship). This trend means that...

Bundling/unbundling

(Products or services) in this industry are increasingly being (bundled, unbundled). This makes it (easier, more difficult) for firms to compete who can't offer all of the bundled goods.

Shift to one-stop shopping

More and more customers are looking for one single source. This gives a huge advantage to firms that offer an extremely broad array of (products or services), but a disadvantage to those that don't. Depending on how much this trend continues, the likely result will be...

Product substitute creating change

The continuing inroads of (the product or service substitute) continues to shake this industry and can be expected to continue to do so for some time to come. Most firms are reacting to this challenge by.... Other firms are..... Still others are... Additional implications of this change include...

Primary competitors

How Do I Get Here?

You should double click on this selection for each of the competitors you will provide analysis on. In other words if you have three competitors you will discuss, double click three times.

Here you should focus on the companies that you compete with--not their particular products or services. Direct your competitive analysis to those few firms that you compete most directly with. Focus in less depth on firms that you compete with less directly.

Include and edit one type of analysis...

Basic competing company analysis

Name:
Location:
Sales:
Profitability:
Number of employees:
Years in business:
Strategy:
Competitive strengths:
Competitive weaknesses:
Other pertinent info:

[See Business Plan Example #17]

Lawn Masters of Newton

Business Plan Example #17

Primary competitors

Name	Green Lawns, Inc.
Location	123 Washington Street
	Newton, MA
Sales	$1.3 million (est.)
Profitability	?
Number of employees	50 (peak)
Years in business	30
Strategy	Full service
Competitive strengths	Large client base
	Offer wide range of services
Competitive weaknesses	Lack of modern management
Other pertinent info	

....

Name	Total Lawn
Location	88 Mt Auburn Street
	Watertown, MA
Sales	$2 million (est.)
Profitability	?
Number of employees	70 (peak)
Years in business	25
Strategy	Full service
Competitive strengths	Large client base
	Offer wide range of services
Competitive weaknesses	Lack of modern management
	Not focused in Newton
Other pertinent info	

....

Name	Landscaping Specialists
Location	78 Boylston Street
	Newton, MA
Sales	?
Profitability	?
Number of employees	65 (est.)
Years in business	about 20
Strategy	Commercial and residential
Competitive strengths	Modern equipment
	Offers top quality commercial services
Competitive weaknesses	Perceived to be oriented toward businesses
Other pertinent info	Owned by holding company with several other similar businesses operating in different parts of Greater Boston

Matrix provides at-a-glance competitive comparisons

COMPETITIVE COMPANY MATRIX

Main competitors: (Company #1)   (Company #2) (Company #3) (Company #4)
Industry rank:
Overall competitiveness:
Estimated sales:
Sales trend:
Estimated profits:
Financial strength:
Apparent strategy:
Product positioning:
#1 Target customers:
#2 Target customers:
Seen by customers as...
Loyalty of customers:
Quality reputation:
Sales strength:
Advertising strength:
Use of promotions:
#1 Strength:
#1 Weakness:
Other key point:
[*See Business Plan Example #18*]

Principle competitor strategy

How Do I Get Here?
  You should double click on this selection for each of the competitors you will provide analysis on. In other words if you have three competitors you will discuss, double click three times.

   Our (#1, #2, #3, etc.) competitor is... They compete largely by (price, emphasizing quality, being a full service provider, reputation, advertising, offering new products, offering service options, being flexible in serving customer needs, an aggressive sales effort, having a particularly strong capability in..., being particularly good at..., focusing on the...market niche, specializing in customers who want...). Their major competitive strength is... They have succeeded in the market because...

Competitive products/services

   Focus your competitive comparison on those few products or services that you compete with most directly. Focus in less depth on products or services that you compete with less directly.

Lawn Masters of Newton

Business Plan Example #18

COMPETITIVE COMPANY MATRIX

Main competitors	Green Lawns	Total Lawn	Landscaping Specialists
Industry rank	3	2	1
Overall competitiveness	1	2	3
Estimated sales	$1.2M	$2M	$2M+
Sales trend	up	steady	up
Estimated profits			
Financial strength	high	?	high
Apparent strategy	Full-service	Full-service	Full-service,
Res. And Com.			
Seen by customers as	Familiar	Outsiders	Business-oriented
Loyalty of customers	High	Medium	?
Quality reputation	Medium	Medium	High
Sales strength	Medium	Medium	High
Advertising strength	Low	Low	High
Use of promotions	Low	Low	Medium
#1 Strength	Service range	Service range	High Quality work
#1 Weakness	Disorganized	Disorganized	Non-residential focus

Our #1 competitor is Green Lawns Inc. They compete largely by being a full service provider. Their major competitive strength is their years and years of full-service delivery in Newton. They have succeeded in the market because they have a local focus and they will agree to do just about anything.

Our #2 competitor is Total Lawn. They compete largely by being a full service provider. Their major competitive strength is their large client base and the economies of scale that offers them. They have succeeded in the market because they operate in several communities and offer a wide range of services.

Our #3 competitor is Landscaping Specialists. They compete largely by emphasizing quality and the most up-to-date equipment. Their major competitive strength is their professionalism They have succeeded in the market because they dominate the profitable commercial services sector.

Include and edit one type of analysis...

Basic competing product/service analysis

(Product/service): _____

Competitor: _____

Unit sales: _____

Dollar sales: _____

Sales trend: _____

How Do I Get Here?

You should double click on this selection for each of the competitors you will provide analysis on. In other words if you have three competitors you will discuss, double click three times.

Profitability estimate: _____

Price: _____

Target Buyers: _____

Primary positioning: _____

_____

Features/attributes most emphasized
in ads/sales pitches or packaging:

1. _____

2. _____

3. _____

4. _____

5. _____

Sales methods: _____

_____

Advertising budget: _____

Advertising themes: _____

_____

Promotional/incentive programs: _____

_____

_____

Competitive strengths: _____

_____

_____

Competitive weaknesses: _____

_____

_____

Other pertinent info: _____

_____

Matrix provides at-a-glance competitive comparisons
COMPETITIVE PRODUCT/SERVICE MATRIX

	(Product #1)	(Product #2)	(Product #3)	(Product #4)
Product/service:				
Price:				
Estimated sales:				
Sales trend:				

Target customers:
Main features:
Secondary features:
#1 selling point:
#2 selling point:
#3 selling point:
#4 selling point:
Relative quality:
Relative reputation:
Loyalty of customers:
Advertising support:
#1 Strength:
#1 Weakness:

Principle competitive product/service positioning

How Do I Get Here?

You should double click on this selection for each of the competitors you will provide analysis on. In other words if you have three competitors you will discuss, double click three times.

The (name product or service) competes with us (head-on, directly, directly for some customers, indirectly). It is positioned as (having outstanding quality, being the low price option, having the best engineering, being the most technically advanced, being specialized for..., being a highly customized solution, providing a high level of service, offering the best personalized service, serving the following market niche..., being a recognized brand name, being the market leader, being the most innovative product, being the most professional, being the best option for customers who...). Customers appear to (accept, agree with, not agree with, not be aware of, not care about, not give much attention to, disagree.) with the company's intended positioning of it's (product or service). (Instead customer's view this product or service as...)   The major competitive strength of this (product or service) is... Its major weakness is...

Opportunities

Compare markets, customer needs, and customer characteristics with competitive offerings to help determine market opportunities. Include all major opportunities that you think might exist, not just those you are most likely to pursue. This will help open your mind to new opportunities and make your plan more complete for future reference and for showing to outside investors or advisors.

Include and edit all of the following that apply...

Basic unfilled needs statement

Based upon an evaluation of the market, buyers needs and current competitive offerings, we feel there is an unfilled need for a (product or service) that... This (product or service) would be particularly desired by buyers who...   Current offerings, such as...partially meet the needs of such buyers, but a new (product or service) that addresses their needs more directly would clearly appeal to some buyers of current options.

Filling a need better

While there are many different (product or service) attributes that matter to buyers, (describe feature/attribute) is particularly important to them. While competing offerings include this feature, we believe there is significant room for improvement in it--and more importantly that such improvement would have a very strong attraction for buyers.

Finding a niche

Most buyers needs appear to be fairly well served by current (product or service offerings that are generally directed toward the needs of the largest portion of the market which is most concerned with... However, some buyers who are more concerned with... are not being well-served by current product offerings.) We believe there is a terrific opportunity for a (service or product) that meets the needs of these buyers directly.

Serving a new/different market

While the competition is well-established in, and gives a lot of focus to, current major markets for this product, they are much less aggressively pursuing the (enter emerging market) market. This market offers terrific potential because it has significant growth potential, and the competition is not well-entrenched here. Furthermore, this market differs from the other markets in the following important ways.... While this market may not be the largest, it appears a very solid opportunity for a less established competitor.

Opportunities in competitor's weaknesses

An examination of the competitive offerings finds several weaknesses. The most important weakness is... This weakness is particularly important because it is of major concern to many buyers. Other weaknesses include... A (product or service) that was able to overcome some of these weaknesses, for example by..., would rapidly gain a solid market position. [*See Business Plan Example #19*]

A new competitive focus

Many industry participants are well-entrenched with solid market positions. The nature of the competition is overwhelmingly focused on.... While this focus is relevant for the needs of most buyers, it tends to overlook and downplay other important needs of buyers such as... So a new (product or service) that focuses on... will clearly stand out from the competition and quickly get the attention of buyers.

One competitive edge

After reviewing the currently successful (products or services) in this marketplace, it is apparent that all of them do a relatively good job of addressing the following basic needs of buyers.... A new product or service would have to also meet these needs as well as the competition does. But to stand out from the pack and give buyers a reason to go with a new

Lawn Masters of Newton

Business Plan Example #19

Opportunities

An examination of the competitive offerings finds several weaknesses. The most important weakness is the fragmentation of services offered. Some firms only mow lawns and prune shrubs. Others only do re-seeding and care for new lawns. Still others specialize in weed and pest control. Such fragmentation makes one-stop shopping difficult if not impossible. This weakness is particularly important because it is of major concern to many buyers – they want one company to do exactly what they need, no more, no less. That is the role we intend to play.

In addition, we do not feel that most of our competitors run their businesses as efficiently as possible. We will be the only service organization in Newton, for instance, to schedule crews by computer, to communicate with the field via mobile communications technologies, to have serious staff training programs, and to offer customer feedback and evaluation through our Internet web page.

offering, a new product needs to be very clearly superior in serving at least one of these basic needs. The needs that offer the best opportunity for superior performance are... [*See Business Plan Example #19*]

Several possible options

After reviewing the current marketplace, customer needs, and the competitive situation, we are able to identify (two, three, etc.) viable options for competing. One option would be to... The advantages of this option would be... The disadvantages of this option would be... This option (would or would not) match our capabilities well because... A second option would be to... The advantages of this option would be... The disadvantages of this option would be... This option (would or would not) match our capabilities well because... A third option would be to... The advantages of this option would be... The disadvantages of this option would be... This option (would or would not) match our capabilities well because...

Threats & Risks

Identify the most significant risks the business faces. You may want to include competitive threats, possible adverse market changes, major challenges from new products/services, competition reaction to your moves, changes in the industry and changes from outside the industry--such as the introduction of a product or service substitute. If you are raising money from outside sources, especially for equity investment, not adequately disclosing possible risks may be grounds for a lawsuit if the business does not succeed.

Include and edit all of the following that apply...

Basic threats statement

Threats that pose significant risks to our business include... The implications of these threats is... The likelihood of these threats materializing is... We could respond to such threats by...

Start-up risks statement

The business faces the normal risks faced by any business, the uncertainty inherent in a (start-up, new, young) business, the risks common to firms in this industry (such as..., most notably..., of particular concern...), and the following risks peculiar to this company...

Larger, more established competitors

The company faces the risk of competing with much larger, better entrenched competitors. These firms have established and commanding market shares, large advertising budgets, large sales forces, established relationships with customers, and tremendous financial resources. We hope to offset this risk by...

Breaking into an established marketplace

While our competitive analysis shows that our (product or service) out performs competing offerings, there is still a risk that (buyers will be reluctant to adopt a new product, buyers will not consider a new vendor, that market acceptance may take longer than anticipated). So to help accelerate and increase the likelihood of a successful launch we are (launching a major marketing program as described in the marketing section, making a generous one-time product offer as described in the promotion section, developing an aggressive sales program as described in the sales section).

No proven market

Because we are launching a new type of (product or service), there are no guarantees that a market exists for it. We believe however that as shown in our customer needs section of this plan that (there is significant demand to make this product/service viable, there is great demand for this product/service, that our new offering will better serve customers' needs than existing alternatives). We have done (customer surveys, focus groups with potential buyers, informal discussions with key buyers, extensive market research, test marketing, comparisons with other similar markets) that confirm our belief that our offering will succeed in the marketplace.

Turbulent, fast changing market

The marketplace that we are targeting is very turbulent and fast changing. We believe that our (products or services) will meet the needs of buyers in the market for the foreseeable future, but this market has been characterized by short life cycles of product and rapid product obsolescence. We plan to be prepare for market changes by...

New products/services

While we do not have current knowledge of such plans, it is possible that a competitor could launch a new (product or service) that would even more directly compete with us than current offerings do. The kind of offering that would be most threatening for us would be...

The competitors that would be most likely to launched such a product are... We would be particularly threatened by such a (product or service) launch because...

Changes in features/attributes

Possible changes or additional features with competitors' offerings comprise a potential threat. The competitors we are most concerned about in this regard are... Most threatening would be the following potential changes... These would be threatening because...

Competitive reaction

It is possible that one or more existing competitors will react to our entrance into this market. Because of their established market positions, a strong competitive reaction could be a formidable threat. The competitive reactions that would be most threatening would be... However, because of our relatively small anticipated market share, we feel a swift competitive response is extremely unlikely, and there is a good chance that the competition may not directly respond at all. If a competitive response does occur, it is most likely to be in the form of a ... The time frame for different possible competitive reactions we estimate as follows...

Competitive reaction unlikely but possible

Because we are a small firm, we do not anticipate a meaningful or prompt reaction to our market entrance from our larger and more established competitors. However, we have developed contingency plans for certain reactions that competitors may make. If competitors lower their prices, we will (match, better, beat by ...%) their move. We plan to watch for other competitive moves such as (special offers, incentives, new advertising initiatives, product upgrades, service changes, etc.) and we plan to react swiftly to any competitive move. Reacting to competitive moves will in the short run hurt our profit margins, but will in the long run preserve our market share. [*See Business Plan Example #20*]

Price drops

The possibility of falling prices in this market is quite real. Buyers have been known to be pushing for lower prices. Some competitors in very weak market positions are likely to

---

Lawn Masters of Newton

Business Plan Example #20

Threats & Risks

We do not anticipate a meaningful or prompt reaction to our marketing initiatives from our competitors. However we have developed contingency plans for certain reactions that competitors may make. If competitors lower their price, we will match their move. We plan to watch for other competitive actions, such as special offers or service changes, and we plan to react swiftly to any competitive move. Reacting to competitive moves will in the short-run hurt our profit margins, but will in the long run preserve our market share.

respond to requests for lower prices first, and this will pressure more established players to at least partially match price cuts. Because we are building into our business plan the expectation of a drop in prices, we actually might be in a better position to weather falling prices than more established competitors.

Advertising attacks

It is possible that current competitors may change their advertising focus in a way that is disadvantageous to us. For example, one or more competitors may... It is possible that given the rough nature of competition in this business, that a competitor may even attack our (product or service or company) by name in their advertisements.

Product substitutes

Alternatives to the (product or service) are a potential threat. A few buyers have been shifting some of their budgets to... While the amount of money being funneled into substitutes now is quite small, the substitution trend could accelerate in the future.

Changing industry conditions

Changes in the industry could lead to potential problems. The current trend that is most immediately threatening is... The potentially negative implications of this trend are... Trends that are not particularly threatening now, but may become more so in the future, include... Implications to be concerned are...

Business cycle risk

Sales in this industry tend to go up and down with the general business cycle. While there is no guarantee of how far our sales might decline in a general business downturn, we believe that we will have the capability to withstand a (minor, moderate, substantial, large) business downturn. As our profit and loss projections show, even in our weakest sales projection, with sales off ...% from the likely scenario, we still project (breaking even, a profit of ...%, a loss of only...%).

Legal risks

We face possible legal risks from (government agencies..., changing legislation..., competitors who might claim..., customers that might claim..., suppliers that might...). We intend to minimize this risk by...

Insurance coverage

To limit some of the risks facing the firm we (have, intend to) purchase(d) a wide variety of insurance policies including workers compensation insurance (as required by law), key-person life insurance, product liability insurance, equipment insurance, property insurance, loss of receivables information insurance, business disruption insurance, employment liability insurance, non-owned motor vehicle insurance, and...

This page intentionally blank.

STRATEGY

Key Competitive Capabilities

How Do I Get Here?

From the **Main Menu** click on the Business Plan icon. Select Business Plan Text and click OK. You will then be given the option of working on and existing business plan or starting a new one, select the appropriate option and click OK. [If you choose to work on an existing plan the Open dialog box will appear. Click on the plan you want to work on and then click on the Open button.]

The Business Plan window is now visible (see screen shot 1, next page) with your text options in the top half view and your work area below.

Click on Strategy on the sub-menu bar and the summary text will appear. Double click to select a paragraph from the preformatted text. To edit the text click on the text in the bottom window at the point you wish to edit. All common Windows editing functions are available.

List and describe your firm's major competitive capabilities. Explain why these capabilities are important and how much advantage they are likely to give your firm.

Include and edit all that apply

Basic competitive capabilities statement

In comparison to our primary competitors, we possess key competitive capabilities that will go a long way to ensuring the success of our business. Particularly important are the following key capabilities...

Advantages in particular functional areas

We have a strong competitive advantage in our superior ability in (sales, marketing, production, engineering, service, etc.) Important differences between our capabilities and those of our main competitors are... [*See Business Plan Example #21*]

Advantage of key personnel

We are fortunate to have several highly experienced and talented people in key positions. The expertise and experience that they bring to us really sets us off from the competition. Of particular note is their background in... This gives us the capability to...

Product/service advantage

Our key competitive advantage lies in our (product(s), service(s), product concept, service concept). We have a major advantage in our (design, technology, packaging, cost, capability, quality, ease of use, flexibility, etc.) [*See Business Plan Example #21*]

Better positioned for new trends

We are better positioned than our main competitors to take advantage of new trends in (the market, market segmentation, buyer's needs, customer preferences, the nature of the competition, changes in the industry). The particular trend that will benefit us is... This will benefit us because...

More customer responsive

We have an advantage in our customer-responsive approach to doing business. Other firms give lip service to the importance of their customers, but leave a lot of room to be desired in how far they go to serving their customers. But we (are, are planning on) going the extra mile in serving and responding to our customers.

Technology edge

We have a clear advantage in our technology. This advantage derives from... This contrasts with our competitors who are...

Innovation edge

Being a (new, young, forward-looking) company, we are in a position to adopt new and innovative ideas. Unlike our highly established competitors, we are also uniquely well-suited to benefit from change in the industry. Some specific new approaches that give us a competitive advantage are...

A more professional approach

Our advantage lies in the more professional approach that we bring to this industry. Our management approach and the style of our company sharply contrasts with our main competitors. Examples of this are...

Lawn Masters of Newton

Business Plan Example #21

Key competitive capabilities

We have a strong competitive advantage in our superior ability in overall management. Important differences between our capabilities and those of our main competitors are vastly superior scheduling, staff training, and customer feedback systems. We believe that our highly visible management differences will help make us appear in the consumer's mind to be a more reliable service provider.

Another key competitive advantage lies in the flexibility of our service concept. Potential customers can literally select from a menu of options that covers every aspect of lawn maintenance. There is no dimension of the service we will not provide – none of our competitors can make that claim. Other firms give lip service to the importance of their customers, but leave a lot to be desired in how far they go to serving them. But we will definitely go the extra mile in serving and responding to our customers' needs.

More employee-centered

Because superior employees and superior employee performance means such a difference in this industry, our fresh approach to human resources will mean a significant advantage over our competition. Not just another department, human resources for us is one of the most important pillars of our firm. We intend to go out of our way, every day, to see that our employees needs our served. By doing so, we expect to realize a competitive advantage in almost any work where a human being is involved.

More aggressive approach

Our aggressive business approach will be a significant competitive advantage. Other firms in the industry tend not to focus very much on their competitors, seldom make directly competitive moves, and do not maximize their potential. On the other hand, our firm is much more competitively minded and determined to push hard for all the market share that we can possibly get.

Tightly focused advantage

Our specialized focus is a significant advantage. Our main competitors are (in many markets, targeting several market segments, offering many different products, offering many types of services, shifting their focus frequently..., etc.)   But we are going to target our focus on.... This will allow us to better...

Advantages of being a new business

Being a new entrant into this field has obvious disadvantages, but it also has advantages. We can design our business from scratch and position our business to take advantage of recent changes in the marketplace and our knowledge of the current positioning of the other competitors. It allows us to create a totally fresh approach to business that is more appropriate to today's markets and the needs of today's customers

Advantages in being locally owned

Being a locally owned and operated firm, gives us several strong advantages. We can stay much more closely attuned to the needs of our local market and customers. We can respond much more quickly to the demands of these customers. And we can respond rapidly to competitor's moves as well.

Advantage of being a very small company

Being a very small company with few employees gives us several advantages. Our cost structure is lower than the competition. Our firm can be much more responsive to customers and changes in the marketplace. And we have that extra determination to succeed that comes from being a very small firm. In addition...

Reputation advantage

We have a major competitive advantage in our reputation as (a leader in our market segment, a specialist in ..., an easy company to do business with, a high-quality provider, a low-cost provider, an innovative firm, a technological leader, offering superior service, etc.)

Advantages by affiliation

Our affiliation with... gives us a significant advantage. This affiliation allows us to...

Lower cost structure

A major advantage is that we have a lower cost structure. We have no fancy offices, no big salaries, little overhead, and we can watch every expense very carefully. This allows us to charge lower prices without sacrificing quality and still earn a good profit.

Financial strength

We possess several key financial strengths over our competitors. We (have no debt, have less debt, have more equity capital, have better access to money, have a higher profit margin, have a secondary revenue stream, more diversification, a stronger balance sheet, own our own buildings, own our own equipment, are less seasonal, are less cyclical etc.) The implications of this are...

Well-suited to take advantage of competitor's weaknesses

We are well-suited to take advantage of our main competitor's weakness in... We are able to do this because...

Have better access to the customers

A significant advantage is that we have better access to our customers than do our key competitors. Customers are more aware of our (products or services), more responsive to initiatives that we put forth, and open-minded to new (products or services) that we may offer. This is because...

Key competitive weaknesses

List and describe the major weaknesses that your firm has versus your competitors. Explain the seriousness and depth of these weaknesses, and differentiate between weaknesses that definitely will be an issue, weaknesses that may likely be an issue, and weaknesses that are unlikely to be an issue. If you are using this plan to raise money, you want to emphasize here or elsewhere in the plan how you will overcome or mitigate major weaknesses.

Include and edit all that apply...

Basic competitive weaknesses statement

In comparison to our primary competitors we possess some competitive weaknesses that may limit the success of our business. These are the weaknesses... Of most concern is... We intend to offset this weakness by...

Weaknesses in particular functional areas

We have a competitive weakness in (sales, marketing, production, engineering, service, etc.) Important differences between our capabilities and those of our main competitors are...

We plan to narrow this competitive gap by...

Weakness in key positions

While we have many talented people in key positions, we are less competitive in the (name position). The expertise and experience that is lacking in this position is... We intend to overcome this weakness by...

Product/service weakness

We have a competitive weakness in the (design, technology, packaging, cost, capability, quality, etc.) of our (product, service, product concept, service concept). Implications of this are... We are going to strive to improve this by...

Not as well-positioned for new trends

We are not as well positioned as our main competitors to take advantage of new trends in (the market, market segmentation, buyer's needs, customer preferences, the nature of the competition, changes in the industry). The particular trend most likely to harm us is... This trend may adversely affect us because... We can improve our ability to take advantage of this trend by...

Less customer responsive

We have a weakness in our customer-responsiveness. In some instances other firms are doing a better job of going the extra mile in serving and responding to customers. Our shortcoming lies in... We intend to improve this by...

Technology weakness

We have a technological weakness in that... This weakness derives from... This contrasts with our competitors who are... We intend to mitigate the impact of this weakness by...

Competitors are adopting new innovative ideas

We have a competitive weakness in that some of our competitors are adopting new, innovative ideas more quickly than us. The new approach to doing business that has made the most difference is... We intend to shortly adopt some new, innovative ideas in our business including...

Less professional approach

In the past, our company has suffered from a less professional approach of doing business than some of our competitors. Examples of this include... In order to become a more professionally run firm, we intend to take the following steps...

Less employee-centered

We have been at a competitive disadvantage to some of our competitors, because we have not matched their initiatives in human resources. Specifically they have been using a different business model that places much more emphasis on addressing the needs and concerns of employees. The implications for us have been... In the future we intend to give more emphasis to our management of human resources. Among the steps we plan on taking are...

Less aggressive approach

Some other firms in this industry are competing much more aggressively than we are. Our past approach has not focused on the competition as much. We have not made aggressive competitive moves, we have not responded to competitors moves strongly, and in general we have not gotten too excited about changes in the marketplace or the industry. Implications of this approach are... In the future we intend to compete more aggressively. We intend to carefully track market shares of our key (products or services), to follow our competitors more closely, to respond to our competitors initiatives, and to celebrate our gains in the marketplace.

More tightly focused competitors

The narrow focus of some of our competitors gives them a competitive advantage. Because we are (in many markets, targeting several market segments, offering many different products, offering many types of services, shifting their focus frequently..., etc.) we can not focus our effort as specifically as do some of our competitors. The implications of this have been... We intend to offset this disadvantage in the future by appointing product managers to focus on particular (products, services, markets, market niches, market segments, customer types, customers).

Disadvantages of being a new business

Being a new business competing largely against established firms has huge disadvantages for us. To significantly build sales, we must not just find new customers--we must take customers away from existing firms. Having (no, little) sales we have (no, little) income stream. Other disadvantages are... To be taken seriously as a new firm, we intend to take the following steps (develop a very professional looking corporate logo and letterhead, obtain publicity in key publications serving our market, be visible at important trade shows, develop a polished company brochure, have a major grand opening celebration, etc.).

Disadvantages in competing with large, national firms

Being a small, locally owned firm we have several inherent disadvantages in facing large, national competitors. The larger competitors have economies of scale, large buying power and a brand name identity. For our company, the most problematic of these disadvantages is... We hope to offset this by... [*See Business Plan Example #22*]

Disadvantage of being a very small company

Being a very small company with few employees creates several potential weaknesses. It means for example that all employees must wear several hats. At times we may not be able to give the attention to some aspects of our business that larger firms do. We also do not have deep expertise in all functions. Other potential weaknesses are... We hope to mitigate these weaknesses by...

Reputation weakness

We have a competitive weakness in that our competitors have much more established reputations. In addition to being recognized as established companies, other firms are each recognized for their own special reason. These include recognition as (market leaders, proven

Lawn Masters of Newton

Business Plan Example #22

Key competitive weaknesses

Being a small, locally owned firm we have several inherent advantages in facing large, national competitors – but there are some disadvantages as well. The larger competitors have economies of scale, large buying power and a brand name identity. None of them have successfully penetrated our target market community yet, but they could. The professionalism and flexible service package that currently distinguishes us could be matched by a larger, well-funded national company. If a competitor like this does emerge, we will attempt to overcome them by dramatically increasing our local advertising and stressing our local ties, our in-depth knowledge of the Newton community – and all of the good works we participate in as a member of this community.

specialists in ..., an easy company to do business with, a high-quality provider, a low-cost provider, an innovative firm, a technological leader, offering superior service, etc.) To further establish our reputation we intend to...

Lack of affiliations

Our competitor's affiliation with... give them a competitive advantage. This affiliation allows them to... We intend to offset this advantage by...

Higher cost structure

In comparison to some of our competitors, our cost structure is a disadvantage. Because of our higher costs of (specify higher costs), our costs are higher than our competition. We intend to work around this disadvantage by emphasizing our...

Financial strength

Our financial position is a relative weakness. Our competitors have (no debt, have less debt, have more equity capital, have better access to money, have a higher profit margin, have a secondary revenue stream, have more diversification, have a stronger balance sheet, own their own buildings, own their own equipment, are less seasonal, are less cyclical etc.) The implications of this are... We intend to limit the weakness of our relative financial position by...

Well-suited to take advantage of competitor's weaknesses

Some of our competitors are well-suited to take advantage of our important weakness in.... We intend to counter this by...

Less access to customers

Our competitors have better access to customers than we do. Customers are more aware of their offerings, more responsive to initiatives that they make, and more open-minded to new (products or services) that they may offer. This is because they are (more established than us, have had longer relationships with customers, have on-going relationships with these customers, are seen as a less risky alternative, have a better reputation for..., are viewed as more likely to be successful, are seen as more prestigious, etc.) Implications of this are... We intend to mitigate this weakness by...

Strategy

Your strategy is the unique formula for success that forms the foundation of your business plan, as well as governing day-to-day operations. This strategy is not a definition or summary of pertinent markets, but instead, it is an account of the one or two key factors that distinguish your firm from your competitors, and is most expected to contribute to your firm's long-term success. If you are creating a highly detailed plan for an existing business, you may want to also list secondary strategies--but this is certainly not expected in a plan to raise money and your two strategies need to compliment one another so that you are not sending your business in two different directions.

Include and edit the statement that best applies.

Basic strategy statement

Our strategy will be to .... Key elements of this strategy are... This strategy will be particularly effective in meeting the following customer needs... This strategy will clearly distinguish us from the competition, help us get attention from customers, and quickly build our sales. This strategy takes advantage of our competitive strengths because... [*See Business Plan Example #23*]

Outstanding in one function

Our strategy is to build a (sales, marketing, production, engineering, service, etc.) -driven organization. While our company will become recognized as highly competent in all areas of its business, we intend to be recognized as the clear leader in the (sales, marketing, production, engineering, service, etc.) function. We intend to go all-out in (function) to insure our success. We will continue to hire top people in this area, be sure that senior management is actively involved and supportive of it, and when necessary cut expenses in other areas first. We believe that truly outstanding excellence in this area will clearly distinguish us from other firms in the industry and will provide the best opportunity for building and maintaining a leadership position. This strategy takes advantage of our competitive strengths because...

Product/service based strategy

Our strategy is based around the highly (distinctive, unique, superior, differentiated, customized, personalized) (product or service) that we offer. Our strategic advantage lies in our (design, technology, packaging, cost, capability, quality, etc.) We intend to maximize the benefit of this strategy by...

Lawn Masters of Newton

Business Plan Example #23

Main Strategy

Our strategy will be to offer the best, most highly personalized service in the marketplace we serve. Especially being a very small, owner-operated company, we intend to use this to our advantage to be absolutely certain that every one of our customers receives excellent service. We will go out of our way to make sure our customers know that they truly matter to us. We intend to be very flexible in the way we provide service, and to do whatever we can to accommodate our customer's needs. Employees who deal with customers will be carefully trained and will be given wide latitude for insuring that customers are always satisfied.

Implementing this strategy means building a broad line of services to meet a broad range of needs for our customers. The market trend is towards one-stop shopping. Currently customers are increasingly giving a larger share of their business to vendors who provide multiple services. And vendors who have the broadest product lines have the most advantage in working with customers in the lawn maintenance field. This strategy is also one of the fastest and strongest ways that we can differentiate our company from the competition.

We understand that we will be setting a new standard of customer service. We are going to go well beyond the definitions of old and take customer service to a new level. In addition to just plain treating customers well and being responsive to their needs we are going to provide additional services to customers. Initially these new services are going to include on-line feedback and scheduling of special services via our website, and a completely non-toxic, non-chemical option to weed treatment problems.

The best, personalized service

Our strategy will be to offer the best, most highly personalized service in the marketplace we serve. Especially being a very small, owner-operated company, we intend to use this to our advantage to be absolutely certain that every one of our customers receives excellent service. We will go out of our way to make sure that our customers know that they truly matter to us. We intend to be very flexible in the way we provide service and to do whatever we can to accommodate our customer's needs. Employees who deal with customers will be carefully trained and will be given wide latitude for insuring that customers are always satisfied. [*See Business Plan Example 23*]

Niche market focus

Our strategy is to focus 100% of our efforts on the (market niche). By focusing all of our effort and energy on this particular niche, we expect to quickly develop and maintain a leadership position. While other firms try to be all things to all people, we believe that our singular focus will give us significant advantages. Most of the firms serving this niche now also serve much larger markets and give only secondary attention to the (market niche). On the other hand, our firm will give our total focus to this niche; our key executives will stay in personal touch with customers in this niche; and we will be able to respond to changes in this market much faster than our competitors.

New market focus

Our strategy is to focus on the (new market) for this (product or service). While the other markets for this product are already fairly well developed and the competitors fairly well established, we believe that we will have a significant advantage by being the first company to aggressively develop this (new market). This strategy plays well to our competitive strengths and weaknesses because, being a new firm, we would be at a disadvantage competing in already established markets for this (product or service). But because the established firms are focusing a lot of attention on the currently larger markets for this product, we may at least initially have an advantage by focusing intently on the new market.

Specialized product/service strategy

Our strategy is to have a specialized focus (one, two, very few, a highly limited number, one related line of, etc.) (products or services). By concentrating all of our energy and resources we believe we will be able to be highly competitive. Particular benefits from this specialized focus are...

Product proliferation strategy

Our strategy is to build a broad line of (products or services) to meet the full range of our customers' needs. The market trend is toward one-stop shopping. Currently customers are increasingly giving a larger share of their business to vendors who provide multiple (products or services). And vendors who have the broadest product lines have the most advantage in working with customers. This strategy is also one of the fastest and strongest ways that we can differentiate our company from the competition.

Premium producer/service provider

Our strategy is to be the premier (product producer, service provider) in every way possible. We intend to deliver premium quality (products or services) and to run our business in a first class manner throughout. Absolutely everything about our business will be top notch, and our marketing strategy will be to communicate our premium quality to all possible customers.

Low-price/low cost strategy

Our strategy is to compete on price and be the value leader in our field. Given the high level of competition in our industry and the increased difficulty of potential consumers to clearly differentiate among the offerings of different firms, we are convinced that more and more purchase decisions will be based primarily on price. We intend to be the low price leader. And we intend to be able to do so while still realizing above average profit margins, without sacrificing quality. To do this, we intend to have a low cost focus throughout our operation. In addition to keeping costs down, we intend to streamline our focus to have a relatively narrow line of (products or services). Also we intend to leave out many of the features and options that raise the cost of doing business but add only marginal value to consumers. This is a natural strategy for us because we do not have an established brand identity, and it would be difficult for us to develop a reputation that allowed us to command a superior price. But our cost structure is among the lowest of our main competitors, and with a little effort, we may be able to lower it still further.

Name brand strategy

Our strategy is to build a brand identity. The brand will stand for... Our (product or service) plan and our marketing plan will all support this name brand strategy. By developing a name brand we will be able to charge premium prices for our (product or service) and at the same time develop a stronger identity with customers than by simply developing a premium product, but without branding it.

Generic alternative strategy

We will not spend any effort at all developing a brand identity. Instead we will focus on lowering our costs and delivering our (product or service) at the lowest possible price. This strategy will be particularly important given our market analysis, which shows a large portion of customers make their buying decisions based overwhelmingly on price.

Market share leader

Our strategy is to be the market share leader. We shall monitor our competitors closely. We shall match, if not beat, all major moves by competitors. We shall move quickly to restore any losses in market share such as by increasing advertising, upgrading our (products or services), using promotional incentives, or lowering price. This strategy may involve short-term sacrifice of profits at times, but we believe the long-term potential of this market more than makes up for this potential risk. We are particularly well-suited for this strategy because...

Industry innovator

Our strategy is to adopt innovative and leading-edge techniques to all aspects of running our business. Being a younger, smaller company than our competitors, we will have a natural advantage of being able to become recognized as the industry innovator. We have much less invested than our competitors in the past way of doing business, so we have little to lose and much to gain by doing business differently. We want to particularly be recognized as using innovative ideas to directly benefit our customers, such as new policies on pricing and service. But we also want to try innovative techniques for running our business better internally. Because so many of the firms in our industry are seen by customers as doing business "the same old way" and taking their customers for granted, we expect to quickly develop a highly favorable reputation as an industry innovator.

Leading response to one particular trend

Our strategy will be built around the new trend (in our market, in our market segment, in our area, in our industry, among our customers) to ... We will respond to this trend by... By being one of the first companies to take these steps, we will be seen as a progressive leader, on the cutting edge of change, looking for new ways to serve customers, and do business better. Implications of this will be...

Most professional

We intend to be a stand-out in our market as the most professionally operated firm. Especially in a field filled with small "mom and pop" operators who run their businesses in a casual way, we intend to bring a new level of professionalism to this field. We are going to plan our business very carefully; have rigorous hiring and training programs; have specific policies and standards for serving customers; and carefully monitor the quality of our service. We are also going to carefully communicate and market to our customers the key differences and advantages in doing business with us, as opposed to with the competition. We will be sure that our target customers know that choosing us as a supplier is the safe choice for consistent, high quality service.

Numbers driven strategy

Our strategy is manage our business more aggressively and systematically than our competitors by rigorously focusing on the numbers. We will operate with highly specific sales, cost, and profit targets for our company as a whole, and for each department. As much as possible, we will have very specific goals for individuals, too. We will share important cost and sales information with employees. And more importantly we will share profits. Sales people will work according to closely monitored goals, production will be managed according to a tightly managed budget, and everyone will help us minimize overhead. As much as possible we will urge employees at all levels to play an active role in boosting sales, lowering costs, and ultimately increasing profits. By carefully managing the business with an extra focus on the numbers, we intend to become the most profitable business of our size in this market.

Balance between stakeholders

The key difference between us and our competitors is that we are going to give equal focus to specifically aiming to give just as much attention to serving our customers and our employees, as we do to reaching profit goals. By striving to serve all three equally, we believe that we will also ultimately best serve the interests of each group individually. We intend to go way out of our way to take care of our customers. This may mean that we don't make always make a profit on that customer today--but ultimately we will more than make up for it by repeat business from the customer and goodwill throughout the industry. We also intend to go out of our way to take care of our employees. Not just in terms of offering good compensation and benefits, but also in seeing that they have a strong say in how the company is run. Customers and employees are more than crucial to our business. They are our business--and we fully intend to recognize each group as such.

New standard of customer service

We are going to set a new standard of customer service. We are going to go well beyond the definitions of old customer service and take customer service to a new level. In addition to just plain treating customers well and being responsive to their needs, we are going to provide additional services to customers. Initially these new services are going to include...

Superior people in key positions

Our strategy is to insure that we have absolutely outstanding performers in the few key positions whose performance will go a long way to determining the overall performance of the firm. Because so much of one's success in this industry is determined by the abilities of a few people in key positions, this strategy is highly appropriate for this situation. The positions we will focus on are...

Preferred provider to corporations

We will be seen as a premium service provider for larger corporations in our area. While there are many firms in this area providing (service), most are poorly suited or positioned for providing these services to corporations. But because of our experience, our professionalism and particularly because of our exclusive dedication to this market, we will quickly become recognized as the preferred provider for corporations. Every aspect of our operation, from our logo to how our phones are answered, will be designed to appeal to the corporations that comprise our target market.

Technological leader

Our strategy is to be on the cutting edge of technology in our industry. When a company wants leading edge solutions, we intend to be the first name to come to mind. The impressive past technological achievements of some of our key personnel make this a realistic goal. In addition, we will focus on creating an environment suitable for fostering technical advances. Our key development people will be sheltered from the day to day concerns of production issues. And our whole corporate culture will celebrate our technical prowess.

Leadership position in...

Our strategy is to be the undisputed industry leader in (quality, service, personalized service, customization, workmanship, marketing, technology, support, installation, new products, design, fashion, distribution, etc.) To achieve this we will... This will clearly set us off from the competition because... We are well suited to pursue this strategy because...

Affiliation/alliance/partnership strategy

We will pursue (affiliations, alliances, partnerships, strategic relationships, etc.) with companies that... This will give us the advantage of...

Product feature emphasis strategy

We will focus on providing (products or services) that feature (describe the particular feature). Although this focus will limit us to only part of the market, this focus will quickly differentiate us from our competitors. Focusing all of our resources on (products or services) with this feature, we will be able to outperform our competition in this area. This strategy matches our competitive capabilities because...

Strategy by company/customer type

Our strategy is to target as customers, companies that (are in a particular industry, are a particular size, are at a particular state of progress in this area, have a particular need, are in a particular geographical area, etc.) While we have the capability to service a broader range of firms, we are much more likely to succeed by focusing on a narrower range of prospects and by serving them extremely well. By limiting ourselves to companies that meet our criteria, we will quickly expertise in working for these type of corporations, we will develop a word of mouth reputation more quickly, and most of all we will gain an advantage in developing a reputation as a specialist.

Web-based focus.

Our strategy is to base our business on the World Wide Web. While some competitors are beginning to include the Web in their business operations, none have made a whole-hearted effort to make it the center of their business. We intend to do just that. Not only will this differentiate us from our competition, but it will do so in a very positive way. We will immediately be positioned as a high-tech, leading-edge provider. The experience of several of our key employees in development work on the Web makes this a solid strategic choice for us.

Custom solutions focus

Our strategy is to become known as the premier source for customized solutions to difficult problems. By becoming known as the firm that can solve the most difficult and unique problems, firms will be more confident in hiring us for even moderately difficult situations and willing to pay a premium for the extra security in hiring the best. The expertise of our employees makes us particularly well-suited to pursue this strategy.

Marketing-driven strategy

Our strategy is to focus on our marketing. The (products, services) offered by competing companies are similar enough so that customers do not readily distinguish between them based on performance or features. Instead, competition is becoming increasingly focused on marketing and in particular (the sales process, advertising, product positioning, promotions). This is generally how customers and buying decisions are influenced. We will focus our marketing efforts on... We are well-suited for this strategy because... More detail is provided in the Marketing Section of this business plan.

Aggressive sales strategy

We are going to be a sales-driven organization. We will insure that our sales effort is second to none. We are going to go all out to hire and retain top salespeople. We will give extra effort to insure that salespeople are motivated and enthusiastic and will aggressively sell new accounts. We will basically design and run the rest of the business around the sales organization, because the strength of our sales team is what is going to lead this company to success. We are well-suited for this strategy because...

Customer service focus

Customer service is what we're all about. We're going to make sure that our customer service is so good that it really stands out from the competition and gives us a competitive advantage. Clearly customers care about customer service. And none of our competitors are offering consistently superior customer service. To insure that we are more responsive to our customers we will (assign a service manager for each account, offer toll free support, create a customized service plan for each customer, offer ... hour response time, offer on-site service, give a wide variety of service options, offer 24-hour support, guarantee absolute satisfaction).

Limited customer strategy

Our strategy is to limit our customers to those relatively few who meet all of the following criteria... By limiting our customer base, we will be able to design, build, and optimize our entire organization to serving the highly specific needs of these customers better than any competitor. And more importantly we will not get distracted away from the customers that matter. We will be able to give these customers the attention they want, and we will be able to be highly responsive to their needs.

Secondary strategy

Special instruction--select the following statement and then scroll up and select the most appropriate strategy statement to use as your secondary strategy. Most business plans do not include secondary strategies

Our secondary business strategy will be:

Implementing strategy

It's one thing to have a great strategy. It's another to really integrate your strategy into your way of doing business. Beyond the basic ground covered in other parts of this plan, this section gives you a chance to explain specific steps you are going to take to be sure your strategy is really adhered to. If it seems too obvious or is thoroughly covered in other parts of this business plan, you may want to skip this section.

Include and edit all that apply...

Basic steps to implementing strategy

Here are the five basic (steps, changes, initiatives) that we need to take in order to implement our strategy... (obstacles, problems or issues) we are likely to encounter include... We will address these issues by... In implementing this strategy we plan to give extra emphasis to...

Implementation focuses on...

Successful implementation of our strategy needs to focus overwhelmingly on (our products, our services, our engineering, our development, our new products, our marketing, our production, our advertising, our sales program, etc.)   While we shall be diligent in all aspects of implementing our strategy, we will give extra emphasis to this dimension. Particularly important to successful implementation is insuring that....

Strategy implementation timetable

Because this new strategy represents significant changes in our current way of doing business we shall implement it gradually over a period of time, in the following stages:
Stage 1: (describe stage 1) (target date)
Stage 2: (describe stage 2) (target date)
Stage 3: (describe stage 3) (target date)

Getting the company behind the strategy

In order to insure our success, we are going to put the full effort of the company behind this strategy. We are going to be sure that senior employees have a chance to discuss the strategy and offer their feedback if they have not already done so. And we are going to be sure that employees at all levels are aware of the basics of our strategy and keep it in mind as they perform their work. We will launch our new strategy with an all company meeting. When we do our monthly profit and loss and budget reviews, we are also going to spend some time measuring how well our strategy is being implemented. Perhaps most of all we intend to survey our customers to get their input on how well our strategy is serving their needs. [*See Business Plan Example #23*]

Tying compensation into strategy

All too often a great strategy fails to get implemented because people don't really get behind it. Too often employees give first emphasis to increasing sales or profits in the short-term because they feel (either rightly or wrongly) that this is overwhelmingly how their performance is being judged. We are going to change this. We are going to make a significant part of compensation dependent upon how the individual helps the company implement and focus on its strategy. We will take into consideration the employee's contribution to executing the company's strategy in determining (management salary reviews, all salary reviews, performance bonuses, profit-sharing distribution, employee awards).

Implementation in a changing market

Because we are competing in a marketplace and industry where fast and dramatic change is the norm and not the exception, we will evaluate the success and effectiveness of all aspects of our strategy on an on-going basis. It is likely that minor aspects of our strategy or product positioning will change frequently, and it is likely that we will make significant changes in strategic direction from time to time. To promise that our strategy will be static or that it will ideally suit fast changing market conditions would not be appropriate. Similarly we are going to take a pragmatic approach to implementing our strategy for particular products, services, marketing programs, etc. At the same time it is the rapidly changing dynamics of our marketplace that make strategy extremely important, and we fully intend to give the strategic process and its implementation the importance that it deserves.

For new firms only

Being a new firm, we have a big advantage in implementing strategy in that we can start with a clean slate. We can be sure that every new hire is keenly aware of our strategy, from their first job interview, and knows how it should affect their work.

For firms changing strategy

One of our biggest challenges of implementing this new strategy is going to be getting people to change the old way of doing things. Old habits die hard--and we need to have patience and put extra effort into explaining to the people involved why we are changing strategy, why the change in strategy is beneficial, why their role in implementing the new strategy is important, and how they can help us implement it. Implementing this strategy can not just be a one-shot effort, but something that we continually need to remind people about on an on-going basis.

PRODUCTS/SERVICES

How Do I Get Here?

From the **Main Menu** click on the Business Plan icon. Select Business Plan Text and click OK. You will then be given the option of working on and existing business plan or starting a new one, select the appropriate option and click OK. [If you choose to work on an existing plan the Open dialog box will appear. Click on the plan you want to work on and then click on the Open button.]

The Business Plan window is now visible (see screen shot 1, next page) with your text options in the top half view and your work area below.

Click on Products/Services on the sub-menu bar and the summary text will appear. Double click to select a paragraph from the preformatted text. To edit the text click on the text in the bottom window at the point you wish to edit. All common Windows editing functions are available.

Product/service description

First give a brief overall description of your products/services. Then go into more depth on particular attributes and features that are important to buyers or differentiate your offerings from those of your competitors. If you haven't yet launched your product or service, describe the products or services you plan on launching.

Include and edit all of the following that apply...

Basic product/service description

Our current (product or service) can be described as ... The basic purpose it serves for buyers is to ... We first introduced this (product or service) in... Since then we have made the following changes...

Description for multiple products/services

Our current (products or services) can be summarized as... Their overall purpose for buyers can be summarized as... Our most successful offering is... It can be described as... Our second most successful offering is... It can be described as...

Description for multiple product/service lines

Our current product offerings consist of basically (two, three, four, etc.) different lines. The most successful line is... The principle (products or services) in this line are... The next most successful line is... The principle (products or services) in this line are... The third most successful line is... The principle (products or services) in this line are...

List of products/services

These are the principle products we offer ranked in descending order by sales volume:
1. (Product or service)   (optional quick description) $(sales)
2. (Product or service)   (optional quick description) $(sales)
3. (Product or service)   (optional quick description) $(sales)
4. (Product or service)   (optional quick description) $(sales)
5. (All others)   (optional quick description) $(sales)

Description of development progress

Currently we have (one, two, three, etc.) products/services in development. At the time of the writing of this plan the (first product/service) is (almost ready to ship, almost ready to launch, nearing completion, ...% complete, ...% finalized, at prototype, in the research stage, carefully planned out, at the alpha/beta test stage, in testing, ready to go to test market, etc.). Development is progressing well and we hope to (finalize, ship, launch, take to market) this (product or service) in (estimate time). The major steps left to be accomplished are...The other products are at the following stages of development...

Basic product or service with many options

Essentially we provide just (one, two, three, etc.) (products or services) but we offer many different (variants, features, options, etc.)   The basic product (describe basic product)... The most common (variants, features, options, etc.) are... [*See Business Plan Example #24*]

Product/service philosophy

Our underlying philosophy in (developing, making, creating, designing, buying, selling, renting, providing, delivering) (products or services) has been to... Important objectives are to... We insure that we achieve these objectives by...[*See Business Plan Example #24*]

Products and related services

We offer a range of (describe products) as well as provide related services. We try to serve as many needs as possible for our customers in terms of...(describe the types of customer needs you satisfy). Our principle products are... The services we provide are...

Lawn Masters of Newton

Business Plan Example #24

Positioning of products/services

We will position ourselves as providing highly customized solutions to customers with particularly demanding or specific requirements – and in our community, almost every homeowner believes that they have particularly demanding or specific requirements. We will be highly flexible and responsive in adapting our services to the needs of consumers in Newton. The types of buyers who are most likely to benefit from our approach will be single-family homeowners with full acre lots and plenty of trees and shrubs.

Typical local service business description

We are a local service business providing (type of service). We offer the following specific service options... Our customers are primarily from the areas of.... But we also get some customers from... We have been in business for... years. Over the last few years (our customer base has changed, our business has grown considerably, our mix of services has shifted to..., we have changed..., etc.)

A broad range of services

We offer a broad range of services to our customers. We serve (companies ranging in size from...to..., companies primarily in the following industries..., people who are..., customers that seek..., etc.) The common element of all of our services is that... Following is a summary and description of our primary services...

Service described in terms of goals

The goal of our service is to help (people, companies) to better... They engage our services because... We provide help by doing the following... Typical situations that we have (expect to) work in are...

Highly customized solutions

We provide highly customized solutions for companies that need... Companies engage us because of our expertise in... Recent projects have included... The average assignment requires about .... days to complete. Some customers we work with on a one-shot project basis, and other customers we work with on an on-going basis.

General provider with a specialty

We are a general provider of (products or services) for the (describe marketplace). We cover a broad range of needs from....to... We have also developed a specialty in...

Major features

Important features of our (product or service) are... These features serve the needs of buyers by... An important unique feature of our (product or service) is... This is important to buyers because... Other unique features of our (product or service) are...

What buyers find appealing

What buyers have found particularly appealing about our (product or service) is... This allows buyers to... The advantage of this is that...

Unique aspects of product/service

What is particularly unique about our (product or service) is its... This is important to customers because...

Product selection criteria

Product selection plays an important role in defining our business. We select products with great care using the following criteria... We are particularly careful to select products that will... On the other hand we avoid products that... Overall we strive for a mix of products that...

Pricing

Our (product or service) has a (standard, suggested retail, estimated street) price of $... Typically we (offer discounts, rebates, incentives, volume savings, offer specials, hold sales, etc.) to make the average selling price... Our pricing can be considered to be (high, above average, slightly above average, average, slightly below average, below average, low) in comparison to our main competitors.

Revenue break-out

Our revenue break out by (product, product line, service or service line) is...

Product/Service:	Unit Sales:	Revenue:	Percent of Total:
1.			
2.			
3.			
4.			
5.			
6.			

[*See Business Plan Example #25*]

Summary listings of products/services

We offer the following (products or services)...
Name:_____
Brief description:_____
Key features:_____
Sales:_____
Price:_____
[*See Business Plan Example #25*]

Rewards/honors/achievements

We have received the following (awards, achievements, honors) for our (products or services). This honor was awarded for (criteria for prize).

Favorable media reviews/attention

Our (products or services) have received (glowing, positive, encouraging, wonderful, excellent) reviews in the following media... Of particular note is an article that appeared in (publication) that described our (name product or service) as...

Positioning of products/services

In many business plans, the positioning of products or services will be adequately covered in the strategy section and you won't need to address positioning as a separate issue. But if positioning was not already covered, or if you want to discuss it in more depth, here is the place to do it.

Positioning is the art of planning how customers will perceive your products or services versus the competition. Will your products or services be seen as the inexpensive low-end alternative? The high-end premium solution? Will they be seen as the established "safe" bet? An innovative new idea? There are almost an unlimited array of possibilities for positioning your products or services, but the examples here include most of the more common types of positioning.

Include and edit all of the following that apply...

Basic positioning statement

Our (products or services) will be positioned in the marketplace as... They will be targeted at buyers who have a need for a (product or service) that... These are the particular (attributes, features, components, aspects) of our offerings that will be important for positioning our (products or services)...

Outstanding quality positioning

We will position our (products or services) as the quality leaders. We see quality in this market as largely being defined as... Our (products or services) will be seen as offering higher quality than competing lines because of...

Low price positioning

We will position our (products or services) as the low price alternative. We will let buyers

---

Lawn Masters of Newton

Business Plan Example #25
Product/service description

Essentially we provide one comprehensive lawn maintenance service, but we offer many different options, including:

-- Spring clean-up
-- Tree and shrub trimming
-- Fertilizing
-- Mulching
-- Weed control
-- Insect control
-- Mowing
-- Leaf removal
-- Winter prep
-- Seeding
-- Sodding

Business Plan Example #25 Continued

Our underlying philosophy in developing this spectrum of services has been to present ourselves as the one-stop solution for all lawn maintenance needs. Important objectives are to manage each account carefully to lead to profitability and repeat business. We insure that we achieve these objectives by following up frequently to see that every customer is satisfied, and to give them a feedback/evaluation and special services request vehicle at our website.

Our revenue break out (FY '97) by service is:

Product/Service:	Unit Sales:	Revenue:	Percent of Total:
1. Spring clean-up	300	90,000	6.6%
2. Fertilizing & mulching	150	150,000	11.1%
3. Trimming	200	75,000	5.5%
4. Weed control	150	75,000	5.5%
5. Insect control	60	50,000	3.7%
6. Seeding	200	200,000	14.8%
7. Sodding	125	200,000	14.8%
8. Mowing	300	300,000	22.2%
9. Leaf removal	400	120,000	8.8%
10. Winter prep	300	90,000	6.6%
TOTAL		1,350,000	

We offer the following services:

Name	Spring clean-up
Brief description	Remove debris, selective seeding, repair damage
Key features	Tree and shrub surgery optional
Sales	$90K
Price	$300
Name	Fertilizing & mulching
Brief description	Prep for partial or complete reseeding
Key features	Non-toxic chemicals used
Sales	$150K
Price	$1000
Name	Trimming
Brief description	Optional add-on to annual service package
Key features	Flat fee for basic level of trees and shrubs
Sales	$75K
Price	$400

know that they can buy our (product or service) with confidence and that it matches the most important features of competing (products or services), but our central positioning will be price point.

Best engineered positioning

We will position our (products or services) as offering the best engineering. We will particularly emphasize our (reliability, high performance, performance in highly demanding situations, durability, etc.) This positioning is well suited to our capabilities because...

The most technically advanced products or services

We will position our (products or services) as the most technically advanced offerings available today. We will particularly emphasize the (performance, certain features, certain capabilities, state-of-the-art capabilities, etc.) of our (products or services.)

Providing specialized products/services

We will position our products as highly specialized solutions for (the market segment..., buyers who demand..., consumers who desire...). We will target this part of the market exclusively and develop a reputation as a leading provider in this market niche.

Highly customized solutions

We will position ourselves as providing highly customized solutions to customers with particularly demanding or specific requirements. We will be highly flexible and responsive in adapting our (products or services) to the needs of these buyers. The types of buyers we are most likely to benefit from our approach will be...

Products with a high level of service

We will position ourselves as providing a unusually high level of service in combination with our product offerings. While the quality of our products will compare favorably with our competition, it is our extraordinarily high commitment to service that will really distinguish us from the competition.

The best personalized, service

We will position our service as the best and personalized available. Taking advantage of the small size of our company, our devotion to excellence, and our close attention to customer's needs, we are going to build a reputation for the highest quality, personalized service unparalleled in our marketplace.

Serving a niche market

Our (products or services) will be 100% focused on the (market niche). Each of our (products or services) will be (optimized for this market, designed specifically for the needs of this market, tailored for this market, marketed as the best solution for this market, positioned as ideal for buyers who want...)

Brand name positioning

Our (products, services) will be positioned as a brand name, high quality solutions for the needs of buyers in this marketplace. Our brand will quickly assure buyers that they are getting a (product or service) that will... This brand name will be carefully cultivated through a comprehensive marketing program.

Market leader positioning

Because of our high market share, we are in the unique position to present our (products or services) as the market leaders. While there are certain particular attributes and features that we will emphasize in marketing from time to time, we are first and foremost going to position our (products or services) as the market leaders that they are. Many buyers have shown their preference to go with the (product or service) that they believe is the market leader even when it commands a slightly higher price--so we believe that this is a particularly powerful positioning strategy.

Most innovative positioning

Our (products or services) will be positioned as the most innovative solutions in the marketplace. Some of the types of innovations that we will initially emphasize are... Being a younger, smaller company than our competitors we have a natural advantage of being able to be recognized as the industry innovator.

Most professional positioning

We intend to have our (products or services) stand out in the marketplace as the most professionally delivered solutions available today. Especially in a field filled with "mom and pop" operators who run their businesses in a casual manner, we intend to position our (products or services) as the professional alternative. Not only will we offer more consistent and higher quality solutions--but our marketing strategy will clearly communicate these differences to our potential customers.

Positioned for certain company/customer type

We will position our (products or services) as designed for companies that (are in a particular industry, are a particular size, are at a particular state of progress in the area, have a particular need, are in a particular geographical area, etc.) While without too much effort our (products or services) could be sold to a broader range of firms, we want to clearly position our (products and services) for this narrower range of prospects. By doing so we will position our (products or services) as specialized solutions.

Positioned for certain consumers

We will position our (products or services) for consumers who (are in the age group of..., have the following lifestyle characteristics..., are male or are female, have an income in the range of..., work in the ... profession, live in ..., partake in the following type of activities..., etc.)

Positioned by affiliation

Our (products or services) will be positioned by our affiliation with... We will reflect this affiliation in our (product or service name, in our packaging, in our advertising, in our literature, in our sales calls, in cross promotions with the affiliated organization, etc.)

Multiple positioning strategies

Each of our (product/service) lines will be positioned distinctly to allow us to capture as much of the market as possible and minimize the degree to which our lines compete with one another. Each line will be positioned as follows...

(Product/service line #1): (Positioning)
(Product/service line #2): (Positioning)
(Product/service line #3): (Positioning)

Competitive evaluation of products/services

Especially for plans for a new business, I would skip this section--it's hard to evaluate products or services that don't yet exist.

Give your first focus to the most important competitive differences. Then if you want to get into more detail, work your way through the less important competitive differences going into less depth as you get further away from the major issues.

Include and edit the one or two statements that best apply...

Basic competitive evaluation statement

Overall in comparison to the offerings of other firms, our (products or services) are (excellent, above average, slightly above average, average, slightly below average, well below average, weak). Our primary (product or service) strengths are... Are primary (product or service) weaknesses are... The weakness that we should give first focus to improving is... We can improve this aspect by...

Quick competitive summary of your product/service

Either rank each entry from 1 being the lowest to 10 being the highest
or rank each item: Excellent, good, above average, average, below average, weak.
This is a quick summary of how our (product or service) compares to our main competitors on key dimensions:
Product/service:...
Market share...
Sales trend...
Profitability estimate...
Price...
Clarity of positioning...
Overall quality...
Overall value...
Reputation...
Distribution...
Packaging...
Sales force ability...

Advertising program...
Promotional program...
Customer service/support...
Guarantee/warranty...
Feature #1 (specify feature)...
Feature #2 (specify feature)...
Feature #3 (specify feature)...
Feature #4 (specify feature)...
Feature #5 (specify feature)..

Rank each of the following product/service attributes relative to the competition Ranking versus competition for this product/service....
(5=excellent, 4=above average, 3= average, 2=slightly below average, 1=weak).

Overall quality...
Competitive pricing...
Clear target market focus...
High level of service...
Most personalized service...
Name recognition...
Most innovative...
Most professional...
Engineering/design...

The top five strengths
For our (product or service) our top five competitive strengths are:
1. _____
2. _____
3. _____
4. _____
5. _____

The top five weaknesses
For our (product or service) our five most serious competitive weaknesses are:
1. _____
2. _____
3. _____
4. _____
5. _____

Competitive analysis for our best-selling products/services

For each of our best-selling (products or services) these are our main competitive strengths and weaknesses:

1. (Product/service)   Main strength: Main weakness:
2. (Product/service)   Main strength: Main weakness:
3. (Product/service)   Main strength: Main weakness:

4. (Product/service)   Main strength: Main weakness:

5. (Product/service)   Main strength: Main weakness:

Increasing competitiveness

In order to make our (products or services) more competitive, we intend to... By taking these steps, we should improve our competitive standing on this issue of... from... to... we expect these changes will have a (huge, large, substantial, significant, slight, marginal) improvement in our sales.

Addressing weaknesses

The most serious competitive weaknesses we face are (weakness #1) and (weakness #2).. At this time, we are not going to address (weakness #?) because (it is less pressing, it would be too difficult to focus on, it would be too expensive to change, the outcome of working on this issue would be uncertain). Instead we are going to focus on improving (weakness #?). We intend to address this by...

Competitive gap

In comparison to competitive (products or services) the most threatening competitive gap that we face today is ... We (will, will not, may) be able to narrow this gap in the foreseeable future. To do this, we would have to... This appears that it (would, would not, be a worthwhile expenditure).

Competitive comparison of success of positioning

Customers appear to (accept, agree with, disagree with, not accept, question, are not sure about) how we are trying to position our product/service. Instead, our customers perceive our (product or service) as being... Other companies (have been successful, have not been successful, have had mixed results) in successfully positioning their (product or service) in the mind's of customers. Companies that have been particularly successful are... They have succeeded at this by... In order to be more successful in positioning our (product or service) we should...

Future products/services

Here discuss not just potential new products/services, but also changes that you might make to your current products/services. Go into detail only if your plans for future offerings are relatively firm.

Include and edit all of the following that apply...

Basic future product/service description

We are (doing feasibility studies of, researching, planning, working on a prototype, nearing production on, getting ready to release, getting ready to deliver) (describe new product or service) The basic purpose it will serve is for buyers to ... We plan to introduce this (product or service) in... We will first market it to... The key differences with this future (product or service) and our current (product or service) is... The impact of this new (product or service) on the company will be...

Product/service improvement/changes

We intend to (improve the quality, improve the functionality, improve the versatility, improve the packaging, upgrade the image, lower the price, increase the selection, expand the variety, etc.) of our (services or products). We will do this by making the following changes... An important implication of (this or these) change(s) is...

Major new product/service

We aim to launch a major new (product or service) that will significantly boost our revenues. By launching this new (product or service) we hope to achieve... Important characteristics of this new product will be... This new (product or service) will differ from our current offerings in that...

Product/service upgrades

We intend to (upgrade, revise, update) (all of our, our leading, our best-selling, our most popular) (products or services) at least every (months or years). Upgrades will typically involve... Upgrades are an important way to make our (products or services) appear current without the expense of an entirely new offering, to stay competitive with other firms, and to get the attention of potential buyers.

Product/service launches

We aim to launch (enter number) major new products per year. Common attributes of these (products or services) will be... In order to achieve this number of new (product or service) launches it is particularly important that we (increase the staff, increase the advertising budget, add salespeople, move to a larger facility, obtain additional financing, increase our customer service staff). [*See Business Plan Example #26*]

Improve performance

We will improve the performance of our (product/service) as measured by (measurement means). We will achieve this by... Currently on this criteria we (are on a par with, are slight-

---

Lawn Masters of Newton

Business Plan Example #26

Future products/services

We are planning a new service, to be launched next year (1999), which can be described as a local supply and support center for homeowners who wish to do some of their own yard work. Specialized tools and equipment will be available for purchase or rental. Top soil, fertilizer, sand, and stones of various sorts will also be available. This support center will complete our goal of offering some product or service for every aspect of lawn maintenance, including the do-it-yourselfers.

ly behind, are well behind, are slightly ahead of) our competitors. After these steps are taken we hope to significantly outperform our competitors in this area.

Competitive feature response

We will match every major feature that our principle competitors add to their (products or services) within (enter amount) months. To do this, we will monitor their offerings closely and respond promptly to any significant enhancements they make.

Competitive price response

We will match every price decrease or special offer that our competitors offer and we will seek to reduce our costs to offset any decrease in margin. We will not let our competitors use price as a tool to increase market share.

Shift product/service mix

We intend to shift our product mix so that (...% of our sales come from new products; ...% of our sales come from ...product; ...% of our sales come from service; ...% of our sales come from ...customers). By doing this, we will (increase our profit margins, have a stronger foothold in an important growing market, diversify our customer base, decrease our dependence upon our main product, better position ourselves for growth).

Basic change of product/service

We are planning to change our (product or service) in the following way...The basic purpose of this change will be to serve buyers better be.... We anticipate making this change in (month, year) We expect this change to have the following impact...

Change/addition/subtraction of major features

We are planning on (changing, adding, removing) the following major feature(s) of our (product or service) ... These features serve the needs of buyers by... This (is or is not) important to buyers because... We expect the impact of this change to be... We anticipate making this change in (month, date)

No new products/services or changes currently planned

At this time, we do not have plans for new (products or services) or for significant changes to our current offerings. However, we do intend to be responsive to changes in market conditions, customer demands, and competitive offerings. We will closely monitor the marketplace and make plans for changes or new (products or services) should conditions so warrant.

New unique aspects of product/service

In the future we are going to add.... This feature will be unique to our (product or service), and will help further distinguish us from the competition. What is particularly unique with this feature is its... This is important to customers because...

Product selection criteria shift

In the future, we plan on shifting our product selection criteria to... We will give added emphasis to... Our overall product mix will...

Outside vendor selection/management change

The sourcing process from outside vendors will change in the following way... We will change the criteria used in selecting vendors... We will give more emphasis to...

Engineering/design process change

We will change our (engineering, design) capabilities to...We will seek to improve our ability to... We will do this by...

Reputation goal

We will strive further for (quality, high quality, superior quality, reliability, integrity, high technology, speed, efficiency, low prices, unique products, dependable service, fashion trends, etc.) reputation. We will do this by...

Pricing changes

We will change our (product or service) (standard, base, suggested retail, estimated street) price from $...to $... We will (increase volume discounts, increase dealer discounts, decrease volume discounts, decrease dealer discounts, eliminate rebates, phase out promotional offers, cut back on sales, change the base price) to make the average selling price... We will shift our pricing to be (high, above average, slightly above average, average, slightly below average, below average, low) in comparison to our main competitors.

Pro-forma Revenue break-out

We anticipate to have established our new (product or service) in the marketplace by (month, year). By this point in time we expect the following sales and revenue:

Product/Service: Unit Sales: Revenue: Percent of Total:
1.
2.
3.
4.
5.
6.

Summary listings of new products/services

We will offer the following new (products or services)...

Name: _____

Brief description: _____

Key features: _____

Sales: _____

Price: _____

Detailed future product/service listings--
same as template for evaluating competitive products

Addendum to User's Manual for
Adams Streetwise® Complete Business Plan

Some changes have been made to the **Win 3.1/Win 3.11** version
of this product that are not reflected in the User's Manual.

Be sure to review the Read Me File.

1. (Product/service): _____

Pro-forma unit sales: _____

Pro-forma dollar sales: _____

Pro-forma sales trend: _____

Pro-forma profitablitiy: _____

Price: _____

Target Buyers: _____

Primary positioning versus
competitive offerings: _____

_____

Features/attributes to be most emphasized
in ads/sales pitches or packaging:

1. _____

2. _____

3. _____

4. _____

5. _____

Sales methods: _____

_____

Advertising budget: _____

Advertising themes: _____

_____

Promotional/incentive programs: _____

_____

_____

Competitive strengths: _____

_____

_____

Competitive weaknesses: _____

_____

_____

Other pertinent info: _____

_____

Principle competitive offerings: _____

_____

This page intentionally blank.

MARKETING STRATEGY

> **How Do I Get Here?**
> From the **Main Menu** click on the Business Plan icon. Select Business Plan Text and click OK. You will then be given the option of working on and existing business plan or starting a new one, select the appropriate option and click OK. [If you choose to work on an existing plan the Open dialog box will appear. Click on the plan you want to work on and then click on the Open button.]
> The Business Plan window is now visible (see screen shot 1, next page) with your text options in the top half view and your work area below.
> Click on Competitive Analysis on the sub-menu bar and the summary text will appear. Double click to select a paragraph from the preformatted text. To edit the text click on the text in the bottom window at the point you wish to edit. All common Windows editing functions are available.

Your marketing strategy is your program for getting customers to buy your products or services. State the underlying principles or commonalties of all of your marketing efforts. Explain how your marketing program will support your company strategy, and your positioning plan for your products or services. Discuss any particular message that you want your marketing to send to customers. You many also want to identify the key differences between your marketing program and those of your competitors.

Include and edit all that apply...

Basic marketing strategy statement

Our basic marketing strategy is to... Our marketing efforts will emphasize... The message that we want to send to customers is that... We will primarily direct our marketing toward (describe market or types of buyers targeted). We will (exclusively, largely, primarily, equally) rely upon (our sales effort, our advertising, our direct mail, our promotion and incentive offers, etc.) to drive sales ahead. Key differences between our marketing program and those of our principal competitors is...

Consistent Image

We will closely integrate all of our marketing and sales efforts to project a consistent image of our company and a consistent positioning of our (products or services). The image we will present is... We will emphasize (this image) in our sales approach by... We will emphasize (this image) in our advertising by... We will emphasize (this image) in our support materials by...

Change image

A major role of our marketing is to change our image. In the past our (company, products, services) have been perceived as... We want to change how we are perceived in our market-place. We want to be seen as... We will accomplish this by...

Marketing message

The marketing message that we want to send is... We particularly want to emphasize... This differs from the messages of our key competitors who are generally emphasizing... in their marketing.

Supporting company strategy

Our marketing program will support our overall company strategy by emphasizing... This will be reflected in all of our marketing including in our sales efforts, in our advertising, and in our literature. For example... [*See Business Plan Example #27*]

Positioning objectives

A major goal of our marketing is to position (our products, services, company) as.... We want to convince our potential customers to think of us as... We aim to accomplish this by...

Sales objectives

Our marketing objective is to increase sales to $..... by (date). We want to increase our customer base to ... We want to increase our share of the market to... We want to increase sales (in a certain market segment, of a certain product type, internationally, etc.) to ...% of total sales. We want to shift our sales mix to the higher margin (products or services) such as... [*See Business Plan Example #27*]

Target markets

The primary target market for our marketing effort will be... The marketing programs we will direct toward this market is... Secondary target markets are... Marketing programs in these markets will include...

Sales focused marketing effort

Our marketing strategy will be based around an aggressive sales effort. In person sales presentations will be the core of our selling effort. Other marketing activities including advertising and publicity will be geared to getting potential customers to agree to meet with our salespeople. [*See Business Plan Example #27*]

Advertising focused marketing effort

Our marketing strategy will be focused around advertising in (the yellow pages, industry publications, local newspapers, the major metro paper, the World Wide Web, etc.). Our selling effort will consist of responding to inquiries that are generated by this advertising. [*See Business Plan Example #27*]

Database focused marketing effort

Our marketing effort will focus on a limited number of qualified leads that we carefully track. Our information on these leads will be stored in our database. We will market to these leads using a variety of one-to-one type contact including (mailings, phone calls, e-mails,

Lawn Masters of Newton

Business Plan Example #27

Marketing strategy

Our marketing program will support our overall company strategy by emphasizing the flexibility and comprehensiveness of our service offerings, as well as the efficiency and professionalism with which we work. This will be reflected in all of our marketing, including our sales presentations, our advertising, and our literature.

Our marketing objective is to increase sales to $2.5M by 9/15/98, the end of this season. We want to increase our customer base to approximately 1000 homeowners, which would bring our market share to about 20%.

Our marketing strategy will be based around an aggressive sales effort. In person sales presentations, scheduled at the potential customer's home on the weekends or in the evenings, will be the core of our selling effort. Other marketing activities including advertising and publicity will be geared to increasing the receptiveness of potential customers to agreeing to meet with our salespeople.

This strategy will be supported by advertising in the local newspapers, the "Tab," the "Graphic," and the "Chronicle." Our selling effort will consist, in part, of responding to and selling inquiries generated by this advertising.

Our marketing program will have 3 major components, focused on developing qualified leads for sales presentations and on strengthening our image as the most professional lawn maintenance organization operating in the City of Newton.

Program 1: A Referral Incentive program, in which current customers who refer a potential new account receives a rebate on their annual service bill equal to 10% of the annual service bill of the referred account.

Program 2. A Free Service Consultation, which is how the at-home sales presentations will be represented. A well-trained and professionally attired consultant will inspect the potential customer's grounds, give an expert opinion as to any unusual needs, and make an overall recommendation as to an annual service plan.

Program 3. A well-publicized effort to support and work with the Newton Community Gardening organization at Nahanton Park as a gesture of goodwill of contribution to the community.

faxes, etc.) We will add to our qualified lead list by...

Guerrilla, low-cost approach

We will take a guerrilla approach in our marketing, avoiding traditional marketing methods such as expensive advertising campaigns and instead rely on lower cost, more creative approaches. We shall be very pragmatic, and quickly drop any marketing method that does not work and replacing it with new ones.

Overall marketing direction

The overall direction of our marketing is to (support the company's strategy, support the positioning of the company's products or services, rapidly open new accounts, acquire new customers, insure that we achieve our sales goals, increase the visibility of our company in the marketplace, differentiate us from our competition,). We shall achieve this by a cohesive marketing program that emphasizes (our company's unique strengths, our product's unique advantages, our services unique benefits, an aggressive sales effort, the comparative benefits of doing business with our company). Specifically we will...

Marketing program components

Our marketing program will have (2, 3, 4, 5, etc.) major components. Each component will (have it's own specific goal, will be designed to complement and support the other marketing components, be directed at a specific target market, will support our overall marketing strategy of...).

Program 1. (Describe)
Program 2. (Describe)
Program 3. (Describe)
[*See Business Plan Example #27*]

Revamp company image

We will revamp the company's image to appear just as competitive and capable as much larger firms. We will re-do the company's logo, letterhead, signage, and packaging, and have a consistent look for all company communications. We will also develop a new central design theme for our advertising that echoes our new image.

World Wide Web strategy

The world wide web will be a core component of our marketing strategy. We will develop a major Web site that we will promote aggressively. We will accept orders on the site, and we will provide constantly updated information for our customers.

Sales Tactics

Describe the different methods and/or sales channels that you are using, or plan to use, to sell your product or service. Detail any aspect of the sales approach that is particularly important for success. Point out any aspects of your sales tactics that are different than your competitors.

Include and edit all that are appropriate.

Basic sales tactics statement

Our primary sales method is (face-to-face selling, outbound telephone sales, inbound telephone sales, our national sales force, independent sales reps, distributors, wholesalers, through retailers, etc.) A particularly important aspect of our sales process is (generating leads, selecting salespeople, training salespeople, finding independent sales reps, selecting distributors, getting retail shelf space, etc.) We address this by... Our sales tactics differ from our principle competitors in that...

A variety of sales methods

We are going to use a variety of sales methods to reach our target markets as effectively as we can. Our sales methods will vary depending upon the type and size of customer we are targeting.

1. (sales method #1) (type and size of customer targeted) (expected % of total sales)
2. (sales method #2) (type and size of customer targeted) (expected % of total sales)
3. (sales method #3) (type and size of customer targeted) (expected % of total sales)

Lawn Masters of Newton

Business Plan Example #28

Sales Tactics

Our sales process begins when the potential customer responds to our advertising by telephoning us for more information. We have found that rather than providing more information over the phone, our best chance of closing the sale is to arrange an appointment to visit the prospect in person. We have found it is fairly easy to persuade potential customers to agree to see a representative of our company in person. The most difficult part of the sales process however is closing the sale. Closing the sale requires not only knowledge of the service but also strong sales skills. We have found that the unique advantages of our service that are important to emphasize in sales calls are our flexibility and professionalism.

An important part of our sales process is uncovering the key concerns and needs of the buyer-- which often differ from one customer to the next. Because of this it is important to have bright and engaging sales people who can think on their feet and who are also effective in establishing a rapport with their customers.

Senior people in the company will do most of this sales work. This is an important competitive element because customers prefer to deal with the management and they are able to be sure that the company will do everything possible to land the sale and to keep the customer happy.

We will support our sales effort with the following collateral: Brochures, flyers, and testimonial sheets.

Inbound telephone sales

Our sales effort is limited to responding to prospects that telephone our business. At this point the customer is seriously interested in buying a (product or service) of the type we are offering but they have not yet decided from which company they will make the purchase. Many prospective customers will call only two or three prospective providers. Hence there is a high conversion rate of turning inquiries into sales. What drives our sales effort is getting the phone to ring in the first place, which is the goal of our advertising program. In responding to prospective customers on the phone, we have found that it is particularly important to emphasize our (low price, high quality, high service level, years in business, reliability, guarantee, free quotations, fast response, etc.) By emphasizing this competitive advantage we have found we are more likely to land the sale. [*See Business Plan Example #28*]

Inbound telephone leads/face-to-face closing

Our sales process begins when the potential customer responds to our advertising by telephoning us for more information. We have found that rather than providing more information over the phone, our best chance of closing the sale is to arrange an appointment to visit the prospect in person. We have found it is fairly easy to persuade potential customers to agree to see a representative of our company in person. The most difficult part of the sales process, however, is closing the sale. Closing the sale requires not only knowledge of the (product or service) but also strong sales skills. We have found that the unique advantages of our (product or service) that are important to emphasize in sales calls are...

Finding leads/telephone cold calling/face-to-face closing

There are basically three core elements to our sales process--all critical for its success. The first is finding good leads. We generally find leads by... Other sources for leads include...

Finding a good lead list is important because the salability from one list to the next varies greatly. The second core element is telephone cold calling. This is a very demanding process because even the best salespeople in this industry must call many, many prospects to find one who is at all interested. Typically we call about (enter number) of prospects to arrange one appointment. The biggest challenges in cold calling are just to get the decision- maker on the phone and then to get them to really listen to the sales pitch. Salespeople require patience and skill to get past gatekeepers such as receptionists, secretaries, and assistants, or increasingly often, voice mail. The third core element, the face-to-face appointment is important also, because less than (half, a quarter, 10%, etc.) of all appointments turn into sales. It is during the face-to-face presentations that we really emphasize our unique benefits such as...

Face-to-face selling

In-person selling is critical for successfully selling our (product or service). We have found that selling over the phone, no matter how good a presentation you make, is much less effective than in person selling. Key elements in a successful presentation include...

National sales force

Our sales are largely handled by our national sales force. It (consists of, will consist of, will be expanded to) ... salespeople and ...support staff. The salespeople will be based in ... Our national sales force focuses its efforts on (all accounts, our top ... accounts, only the largest national accounts, current customers, ... markets).

Independent sales reps (sometimes called manufacturer's reps)

Independent sales reps are an important part of our sales effort. We (have, will have, intend to have, plan to grow to having) ... sales reps covering the following sales territories... The standard commission rate is... Exceptions to the standard commission rate are... By employing independent reps, we are able to have a highly experienced and talented sales force with established access to important accounts. We minimize our overhead because the cost of independent reps goes up and down with our sales volume.

Distributors

We rely on distributors to get our product to market. We (have, plan to have, are in talks with) ... distributors covering the following (territories, markets, regions, countries) ... The advantages of distributors are many. For one, they have their own established sales forces and regular access to key customers. They have a large number of established accounts and customers do not have to go through all of the paperwork of setting up a new vendor to buy our product. Also, we do not have to collect payment from each account we deal with--only from the distributors.

Retailers

Our products are sold through retailers. The overwhelming challenge in our sales effort is to get stocked on retailer's shelves. We intend to sell to retailers by (a national sales force, independent sales reps, telephone marketing, direct mail, by distributors, through whole-salers, by trade shows, an affiliation with..., by a combination of...) We will support this sales effort with (trade advertising, a targeted trade show presence, direct mail, consumer advertising, special offers to open accounts, co-operative advertising programs, free samples). Key elements in successfully selling to retailers are...

World Wide Web

We use the World Wide Web to sell our (product or service) and to attract new customers. We publicize our Web site (in our literature, in our advertising, with references in the major search engines, with links to related Web sites, by advertising on Web site in...).

Key account focus

Because so much of the market is concentrated at a few major accounts, the core of our sales effort is selling these few companies. While we are certainly pleased to get orders from mid-sized and smaller accounts, we focus our effort overwhelmingly on the key accounts. Being a relatively small company with limited resources, we would rather focus all of our effort on covering a few accounts really well, rather than covering many accounts less thoroughly. Also, the smaller accounts often tend to eventually buy many of the same (products or services) as the larger accounts even without any sales effort.

Sales tactics are very important

In our business, sales tactics are crucial. Often customers will buy a (product or service) that is not the best solution on the market for them, because of superior selling tactics of the selling company.

Sales tactics are not crucial

In our business sales tactics are not crucial. Usually customers will compare the competitive (products or services) carefully, and then analyze and select the best solution for their needs. It is important to have an adequate sales program. But basically the competition is driven by the nature of the products or services, not by the ability or nature of the sales tactics.

Exploring unique needs/benefits

An important part of our sales process is uncovering the key concerns and needs of the buyer--which often differ from one customer to the next. Because of this, it is important to have bright and engaging salespeople, who can think on their feet and who are also effective in establishing a rapport with their customers. [*See Business Plan Example #28*]

Strategic partnership

We have developed a strategic partnership with (company, organization, association) to sell our (products or services). They will (sell our product or service, sell our product or service to their members, provide us with prospect lists, recommend our product or service). In exchange we will (give them .. % of the net receipts, allow them the discounted price of..., pay them...)   This is an (exclusive, non-exclusive, written, verbal) agreement and its term is (...years, ...months, open-ended, indefinite).

Owner or president does most sales

The (owner or president) of the company will do most of the sales work. This is an important competitive element because customers prefer to deal with the (owner or president) and (he or she) is able to be sure that the company will do everything possible to land the sale and to keep the customer happy. [*See Business Plan Example #28*]

New markets

We plan on selling into the following new markets... We (will or will not) use our existing sales programs to service these markets. The sales methods we will use are...

Sales collateral, support

We will support our sales effort with the following collateral (brochures, flyers, video's, computer slide shows, computer presentations, data sheets, specification sheets, testimonial sheets, reprints of press articles, free samples, mock-ups, demonstrations). [*See Business Plan Example #28*]

Sales terms

We will sell (on a cash basis only, for cash, checks with proper identification, and credit cards, for credit, for credit after references are checked). Our terms will be (payment in advance, half down and half upon completion, net 30, net 60, net 90, 2% 10--net 30).

Advertising

Describe your advertising message or theme that you want to deliver. State the advertising vehicles that you will use and why you believe they are the best choice for delivering your message to your target audience. You may want to group and describe your advertising programs by product/service line, by target market, or by selected media.

Include and edit all that are applicable...

Basic advertising statement

The message or theme that our advertising will deliver is... The primary advertising vehicle(s) that we will use is (are) (the local newspaper, the metro newspaper, newspaper inserts, shopper newspapers, flyers delivered to homes, ads on bulletin boards, the World Wide Web, local cable television, television, radio, billboards, signs, etc.) Secondary advertising vehicles that we will use are...Our advertising program can best be broken out by (target market, trade/consumer, individual products or services, product/service line, selected media) as follows...

Unique selling proposition

While our (product or service) has several strong, unique competitive advantages, we will focus on just one in our advertising in order to more clearly distinguish ourselves from the competition in a meaningful way and rather than confuse consumers with multiple messages. The benefit we will focus on is... We have developed the following unique selling proposition (short catchy phrase that captures this competitive advantage in just a few words that customers can easily remember.) that will be an important focus of all our advertising: "..." [*See Business Plan Example #29*]

Using advertising to position products/services

Our advertising will be designed to position our (product or service) as (the leading product or service, the quality leader, the most technically advanced, the most reliable, the low cost alternative, the one-stop solution, the most personalized, the most customized, the best for the ....market, specifically designed for customers who..., affiliated with..., the brand name in the market). We will accomplish this positioning by...

Advertising competitive advantages

Our advertising will stress these following competitive advantages... The ads will communicate these advantages by...

Target market for advertising

Our advertising will be focused at (describe target market). We particularly want to reach potential buyers who...The message we want to be sure to communicate to these buyers is...

Trade advertising

We will use trade advertising to reach (buyers, decision-makers, executives, retailers, wholesalers, dealers, etc.) The objective of our trade advertising will be to (stock up retailers, stock up wholesalers, increase our stocking levels, introduce new products, increase the acceptance of our products, position our firm as...). Our trade advertising will be focused in the following media (list media).

Lawn Masters of Newton

Business Plan Example #29

Advertising

While our service has several strong, unique competitive advantages we will focus on just one in our advertising in order to more clearly distinguish ourselves from the competition in a meaningful way--rather than confuse consumers with multiple messages. The benefit we will focus on is our flexibility; that is, the customizable nature of our service offerings. We have developed the following unique selling proposition that will an important focus of all our advertising: "Whatever It Takes to Let You Enjoy Your Yard This Summer"

The purpose of our advertising is to support our sales efforts. It will do this by increasing awareness of our company and its services. This in turn will make it easier for salespeople to get appointments with buyers and achieve their sales goals.

We will advertise in the following local newspapers: The Tab, The Graphic and The Chronicle. This will allow us to zero in on the Newton market, and help position our firm as being closer to the local community than firms that advertise in more broadly circulated media.

We will also experiment with cable television advertising, featuring short interviews with satisfied customers recorded in their own yards.

Finally, we intend to employ the following low-cost advertising techniques: delivering leaflets door to door, putting flyers on car windshields, leaving flyers at other businesses, and car/truck advertising.

We will run our advertising daily during the early Spring (March and April), and start to scale it back gradually throughout the Summer. Another daily push will start after Labor Day and run through September, focusing on leaf removal and Winter preparation services.

Business-to-business advertising

To reach business customers, we will advertise in the business media. Specific advertising vehicles are (industry publications, industry directories, business-to-business phone books, business magazines, business sections of newspapers, local business periodicals, national business newspapers, business television shows, business radio shows, radio news programs, television news programs, etc.) Our advertising campaign to businesses will emphasize...

Advertising to support sales effort

The purpose of our advertising is to support our sales efforts. It will do this by increasing awareness of our (company, product, service). This in turn will make it easier for salespeople to (get appointments with buyers, get through to decision makers, get their phone calls returned, close sales, achieve their sales goals). [*See Business Plan Example #29*]

Ad agency

We will (hire, engage, continue to use) an advertising agency (name agency if already decided) to (develop our creative message, write our advertising copy, produce our finished ads). We will work closely with them and monitor every step of the process. In selecting an ad agency, we will particularly look for...

Freelancers/outside firms/ad agencies/graphic houses

We will hire (freelancers, outside firms, ad agencies, graphic houses, copywriters) to help us with the following aspects of our advertising (market research, market surveys, concept, copywriting, production, typesetting, recording, taping). Other aspects of our advertising we will do in-house: (market research, market surveys, concept, copywriting, production, typesetting, recording, taping). Our criteria in choosing outside firms will be...

Metro/daily newspaper advertising

We will advertise in the major metropolitan newspaper, (name paper). We will advertise in the (sports, lifestyle, main, local, business, food, real estate, classified, auto, etc.) section of the paper. We will buy (the full run of the paper, in our local region/zone) in the following zones...which cover the following areas... We will advertise in the (Sunday or daily, morning, afternoon, evening) edition. [*See Business Plan Example #29*]

Local/weekly newspaper advertising

We will advertise in the following local newspapers... This will allow us to zero in on the specific market(s) that we are trying to target. It will also help position our firm as being closer to the local community than firms that advertise in more broadly circulated media.

Shopper advertising

We will advertise in the local shopper(s), or free newspaper(s), that is (are) distributed in the following areas... Advertising in shoppers (instead of, in addition to) regular newspapers gives us the advantage of (lower cost per thousand, saturation coverage of every household in the market--not just to paid subscribers, a better environment for the promotion-oriented advertising we plan on using).

Magazine advertising

We will advertise in the following magazine(s). This will us allow to target an audience (describe audience). It will also help position our (products or services) as...

Radio advertising

We will advertise on the following type of radio stations (talk radio, news radio, easy listening, contemporary, country, urban, classic, etc.) We will advertise in the following day parts (morning drive time, evening drive time, lunchtime, mid-day, evening, late night, overnight). We will use (pre-recorded spots, live reads, pre-recorded spots with live intro's, sponsorships, on-site broadcasting, special promotions).

Local cable or traditional television advertising

We will advertise on (cable, local, national, national cable) television (on the following systems, in the following communities, in the following markets, on the following networks, in markets that...) We will advertise on the following channels... We will advertise during the...(days or day parts). We will advertise on the following shows... Our ads will feature (video text, a talking head, our product or service in use, our business establishment, satisfied customers, our major selling benefits, special pricing, promotions).

Yellow pages/industrial directory advertising

We will advertise in the (specify town or region or industry if appropriate) (Yellow Pages, phone directory, trade directory, industrial directory). We will place ad(s) in the following category(ies)...

Direct-mail advertising

We will use direct mail advertising to reach potential customers. We will target our mailings to (specify target audience). We will get our lists of names from (magazine subscribers, associations, phone directories, our own customer lists, mailing list brokers, etc.) We will mail (simple postcards, sales letters, a black and white brochure, a first class four color flyer, catalogs, discount/special offer coupons, etc.)

Inexpensive ad alternatives

We will employ the following low-cost advertising techniques (notices on billboards, handing out coupons, delivering leaflets door-to-door, putting flyers on car windshields, handing out business cards, cross promotions with other businesses, leaving flyers at other businesses, discount toward next purchase coupons, signs on customer premises, car/truck advertising, transit advertising signs, World Wide Web links, chat group on-line discussions, advertisements in invoices or statements sent to customers, advertising on the outside of envelopes, advertisements on the back of business cards). [*See Business Plan Example #29*]

Ad breakout by product/service

We will use the following ad media, for the following products...
1. (Product 1) (Ad Media) (% of total ad budget)
2. (Product 2) (Ad Media) (% of total ad budget)
3. (Product 3) (Ad Media) (% of total ad budget)

Advertising frequency

We will run our advertising (daily, weekly, monthly, continuously, using a see-saw approach alternating between heavy and light schedules, in quarterly blitzes to concentrate our impact once per quarter, exclusively during our peak season of...) [*See Business Plan Example #29*]

Advertising schedule

This is our advertising schedule:
1. (Date) (Media) (size of print ad or number of radio/TV spots) (cost)

2. (Date) (Media) (size of print ad or number of radio/TV spots) (cost)
3. (Date) (Media) (size of print ad or number of radio/TV spots) (cost)
4. (Date) (Media) (size of print ad or number of radio/TV spots) (cost)

Promotions/incentives

Describe any promotions or incentives that you will use to increase the sales of your product or service. Describe the duration and frequency of the promotions, the target audience, and how information of the promotion will be delivered to target customers.

Select and edit all that apply...

Basic promotion/incentive statement

We will use the following promotions and incentives to increase sales of our (product or service): (sales, rebates, special events, exclusive offerings, discounts, frequent buyer cards, new customer offers, give-aways, free trials, guaranteed results, trades, cross promotions, gifts, free samples, contests, charity tie-ins). The promotions will typically be held (daily, weekly, monthly, quarterly, once per season, annually, when sales are slow, when inventory is high, etc.) And they will usually last for about (...days, ...weeks, ...months). We will announce these promotions by... [*See Business Plan Example #30*]

Sales promotions

We will run sales to help build our business. Discounts off our everyday pricing will typically range from...to... Sales will be run (every...days, every...weeks, seasonally, when sales are slow, when inventory is high, to tie in with special events or product or service offerings). Sales will last for (...days, ...weeks, ...months). We will promote our sales with (signs, handing out coupons or flyers, in-store flyers, mailings to current customers, mailings to target customers, newspaper advertising, radio advertising, etc.)

Rebates

We will offer rebates to (consumers, dealers, retailers, wholesalers) to spur our sales. Rebates will be featured (in our advertising, on our packaging, in direct mail to dealers, by our salespeople, in our trade advertising, at point-of-purchase, by our dealers' salespeople). Rebates will be (instantly redeemable at point of purchase, mailed in for redemption). Rebates will typically be for $.... Other conditions that apply are... We will offer rebates (once per year, every season, when sales are slow, to launch new products, when a product is becoming obsolete, when a competitor is gaining on us).

Coupons

We will widely distribute coupons to promote our business. Coupons will offer (...discount, free gift with purchase, free trial, buy one get one free, buy one today get next purchase free). We will distribute coupons (by handing them out on the street, by delivering them door to door, at trade shows, in stores, in our newspaper ads, in co-op coupon books).

Frequent buyer program

We will use a frequent buyer program to build and retain a loyal customer base. Customers will be given a frequent buyer card that will be (marked, entered into the computer) after each purchase. After (2, 3, 4, 5, etc.) purchases they will (get a free purchase, get a ...% discount, get a free gift, get a reward check). We will also use this program to get names, addresses and phone numbers of our customers and to track their purchase histories. This will help us tailor our marketing for customers with specific buying habits.

Giveaways/gifts

We will use giveaways to (attract new customers, to build loyalty with current customers, to get more people to try our product or service, to get more people to visit our business establishment). We will give away (free samples, novelty items, ...) We will promote this give away by... [*See Business Plan Example #30*]

New customer offers

To get new customers we will offer (incentive pricing, discounts, freebies, free product samples, free service trials, money-back guarantees, extra advertising allowances.) We will promote this by (our sales force, by calling on target prospects, by direct mail, through our advertising, by advertising in the following media...). Our new customer promotions will be (an on-going offer, a limited time offer, offered to introduce new products or services,

---

Lawn Masters of Newton

Business Plan Example #30

Promotions/incentives

We will run one major sales promotion as an early sign-up discount during the Month of March. Discounts off of standard pricing will typically run about 5% to 10%. We will promote this sales incentive with coupons and flyers, mailings to current customers, and newspaper and radio advertising.

We will also use giveaways to attract new customers and to build loyalty with current customers. We will give away items which depend on a good lawn – such as croquet sets and badminton games.

We see our world wide web site playing primarily an operations support role – but it will also have some promotional role. On the site we will offer service information, basic information about lawn maintenance, suggestions on how to use our service more effectively, links to related sites, discount coupons that may be printed out, and information on how to reach us. We will promote our web site on all our literature, by listing our web address everywhere our street address is listed such as on business cards and on our stationary, and in our advertising.

We will offer free estimates and evaluations without any obligation. We will use this free offer as an opportunity to familiarize the prospect with our business, emphasize our competitive advantages, and try to close the sale.

designed to help launch our business, offered on a seasonal basis, offered every...months).

Grand opening sale/celebration

To create awareness for our new business we will have a big grand opening celebration. The celebration will last for (...days, ...weeks, ...months). During the celebration we will give away (balloons, cookies, ice cream, coffee, doughnuts, raffle tickets for a free trip to.., chances to win a ..., product samples.) We will offer (special pricing, deep discounts, free gifts with purchase, free estimates, reduced service fees, extended warranties, rebates, etc.) The grand opening will be promoted by (signs, mailings, press releases, media interviews, newspaper advertising, radio advertising, direct mail, handouts, etc.)

World Wide Web site

We will promote our business with a World Wide Web site. On the site we will offer (product information, service information, basic information about our business, suggestions on how to use our product/service more effectively, a wide range of information of interest to potential customers including..., links to related sites, discount coupons or rebates that may be printed out, information on how to reach us, pictures of our product or service). We will promote our Web site (on all our literature, by listing our Web address everywhere our street address is listed such as on business cards and on our stationary, in our advertising, in major search engines on the Web, by getting free links with related Web sites, by advertising on the Web). [*See Business Plan Example #30*]

Contests

We will hold contests to (draw attention to our business, help build awareness of our business, get names of prospects to follow up on, get free publicity for our business, create a sense of fun and excitement about our business). A typical contest will be (guess how many jelly beans in the jar, guess how big our sales are, drop your business card in the box, guess how fast our product can..., enter your name and address on the form) for a chance to win a (free product, free service, free trial service, all expense paid trip to..., a color TV, etc.)

Free estimates/evaluations/trials/tests

We will offer free (estimates, evaluations, trials, tests) without any obligation. We will use this free offer as an opportunity to (familiarize the prospect with our business, emphasize our competitive advantages, try to close the sale, offer special incentives such as..., to try to make the sale). [*See Business Plan Example #30*]

Publicity

Describe the central focus or message of your publicity program(s). State the media vehicles that you will use and why you believe they are the best choice for delivering your message to your target audience. You may want to group and describe your publicity programs by product or /service line, by target market, or by selected media.

Include and edit all that are applicable...

Basic publicity statement

The central message that our publicity will deliver is... The primary publicity vehicle(s) that we will target is (are) (the local newspaper, the metro newspaper, trade publications, business periodicals, specialty magazines, the World Wide Web, local cable television, television, radio, signs, etc.) Secondary publicity vehicles that we will target are... We will pitch the media by (mailing press packets, faxing press releases, sending pitch letters, making phone calls, arranging interviews).

General awareness publicity statement

The main purpose of our publicity is to increase the general awareness of our (product and services). Our publicity is also intended to emphasize our competitive advantages and to inform customers and potential customers of new developments concerning our (products or services) and our business. [*See Business Plan Example #31*]

Emphasis of publicity campaign

Our publicity campaign will emphasize sending press releases, sending press packets, sending product samples, sending video tapes, arranging media interviews, holding press conferences, issuing statements, seeking product reviews. [*See Business Plan Example #31*]

Type of media being targeted

Our publicity effort will target the following media (major daily newspapers, local newspapers, network radio stations, local radio stations, network television shows, local television shows, wire services, national magazines, trade magazines, consumer magazines, newsletters).

Product/service focused publicity effort

Our publicity effort will focus primarily on publicizing our particular (products or services) as opposed to the company as a whole. For every new (product or service) launch we will develop a specific publicity campaign. We will also occasionally send out press releases heralding noteworthy achievements or milestones of our (products or services).

Publicity effort focus

Our publicity effort will primarily be focused as follows...
1. (product or service 1) (target media) (number of press kits or contacts)
2. (product or service 2) (target media) (number of press kits or contacts)
3. (product or service 3) (target media) (number of press kits or contacts)
4. (product or service 5) (target media) (number of press kits or contacts)

Newsletter

We will produce and send a newsletter every (month, other month, quarter, etc.) to promote our company and our (products or services). We will send approximately ... copies to (current customers, customers and prospects, dealers, prospects, the following mailing lists...). In the newsletter we will highlight... [*See Business Plan Example #31*]

Lawn Masters of Newton

Business Plan Example #31

Publicity

The main purpose of our publicity is to increase the general awareness of our services. Our publicity is also intended to emphasize our commitment to Newton and to inform customers and potential customers of new developments concerning our services.

Our publicity campaign will emphasize our involvement with the Community Gardeners of Newton by sending press releases and video tapes, and arranging media interviews. We will target local newspapers, radio stations, and cable television shows.

We will produce and send a newsletter every month to promote our company and our services. We will send approximately 500 copies to current customers, and another 1000 or more to prospects. In the newsletter we will highlight items of interest to people who care about lawn maintenance. There will be an editorial column by the President of the Company, a Q&A feature, tips, short anecdotes drawn from actual experiences in Newton, and updates on our involvement with the Newton Community Gardeners.

Press conference(s)

We plan on holding a press conference(s) to announce... It will be held in (location) on (tentative date). We will mail ... invitations to members of the media and we expect ... people to attend.

PR firm/Ad agency

We will (hire, use) (a PR firm or an advertising agency, name agency if already decided) (to handle our entire publicity effort, to develop and write our publicity messages, to produce our press materials, to create our publicity packages, to contact the media, to arrange interviews for use, to mail press releases). We will work closely with them and monitor every step of the process.

In-house publicity personnel

Our publicity effort will be handled in house by..., who will consult with... Clerical support will be provided as needed by...

Trade shows, business-to-business shows, consumer shows

Describe the kind of events you will attend. Specify the events by name if you are fairly certain which events you will attend. Describe what you will do to promote your organization and your products or services both at these events and before the events take place.

Include and edit all that are applicable...

Basic trade show statement

We will (attend, have a booth at, have a table at, conduct a workshop at, speak at, sponsor) (trade shows, business-to-business shows, consumer shows, conventions, seminars). The shows we are planning to attend are (specify shows by name or location or industry.) [*See Business Plan Example #32*]

Objectives of trade shows

Our objective of attending these shows is to (open new accounts, get names of possible leads, build relationships with current customers, launch our business, launch new products or services, emphasize our unique..., portray our firm as a major player in the...industry, seek independent sales reps, seek overseas distribution, seek distributors, meet with key accounts, provide demonstrations, solve problems for customers, check out competitor's offerings, seek new products or services, keep up industry contacts). [*See Business Plan Example #32*]

Type of display

We will use (a table top, a booth, multiple booths, a meeting room, part of a booth, our distributor's booth). Our basic layout will be a (simple array of our products or literature about our services, a placard that ..., a commercial table top display, a portable exhibit booth, a rented exhibit booth, a custom built booth, a commercially built booth).

Emphasis of display/presentation

We will emphasize our (new products, new services, our unique..., a special offer..., our new customer offer..., our catalogs, our flyers, our relationship with our distributor, a contest..., a promotion...).

Promotion of trade show exhibit

We will promote our trade show exhibit by (buying the list of attendees from the show organizers and direct mailing to them in advance, advertising in trade publications, advertis-

---

Lawn Masters of Newton

Business Plan Example #32

Trade shows, business-to-business shows, consumer shows

The City of Newton sponsors several events that are appropriate for our participation, including a Spring Festival, a July 4th event, and an Octoberfest. All of these events are held on the grounds of the City Hall, and local business are invited to rent booth space and exhibit. Our objective in attending these events is to get names of possible leads, build relationships with current customers, emphasize our unique services, and portray our firm as a major player in the this business in the Newton community.

We will make an effort to gather names of prospects at the show by having a drawing and a guest book. We will follow-up with attendees after the show by phoning to arrange a face-to-face meeting.

ing in the trade show circular, having special show offers, having a special event, mailing invitations to key accounts, having a party at the time of the show, giving away..., getting a good location on the exhibit floor, having a drawing at our booth).

Trade show follow-up

We will make an effort to gather names of prospects at the show by (asking for business cards, having a drawing, buying the list of attendees, having a guest book). We will follow up attendees after the show (by phone, by phoning to arrange a face-to-face meeting, by e-mail, by fax, by mail, by sending a sample). [*See Business Plan Example #32*]

This page intentionally blank.

OPERATIONS

Key Personnel

Investors and lenders make their decisions on the basis of people. They especially want to see people who have a proven track record or highly relevant experience. It all starts with the person in charge. You will need to assure everyone who may become involved with the venture that the person running the business knows what he or she is doing and has what it takes to make money. After making these points, go on to describe the other key people. Your management team should have experience in the most important functional areas of the business. Attach detailed resumes for all key personnel in an Appendix. If you are running an existing business you know the key people well, but it may be useful to take an arm's length view of their abilities by summarizing them in writing. Are the right people in the right positions? Should major or minor responsibilities be re-assigned?

How Do I Get Here?

From the **Main Menu** click on the Business Plan icon. Select Business Plan Text and click OK. You will then be given the option of working on and existing business plan or starting a new one, select the appropriate option and click OK. [If you choose to work on an existing plan the Open dialog box will appear. Click on the plan you want to work on and then click on the Open button.]

The Business Plan window is now visible (see screen shot 1, next page) with your text options in the top half view and your work area below.

Click on Operations on the sub-menu bar and the summary text will appear. Double click to select a paragraph from the preformatted text. To edit the text click on the text in the bottom window at the point you wish to edit. All common Windows editing functions are available.

Select and edit the statement(s) that best applies

Basic management team statement

Our management team includes (# of) individuals whose combined backgrounds represent ... years of professional experience in the (relevant field). The President, (Name), has an excellent reputation in the field, and is particularly well-known for (prior successful activity). (He/she) will be directly involved in all aspects of the business on a daily basis, including management of the (functional area) and (functional area) areas of the company. The (Title), (Name), will work closely with the President and will concentrate primarily on the (functional area). (He/She) was chosen for this position due to (his/her) demonstrated expertise in (area of expertise). A third key manager, (Name), will serve as (title) and have primary responsibility for (functional area). Resumes of all key members of the management team follow.

Management & Personnel Structure

The Company will be managed by the (# of) founding partners, whose individual areas of expertise cover all of the functional aspects of the business. (President's name) will serve as the President of the Company, and will be responsible for (functional areas). (Name) will be the (Title) of the Company, in charge of (functional area). The (title) of the Company will be (Name), overseeing (functional area). These key positions will be supported by a full-time staff consisting of (# of) employees, working in the areas of (functional area), (functional area), and (functional area). In addition, part-time staff and independent contractors will be utilized to accomplish several operational functions, including (functional area), (functional area), and (functional area).

Only one key employee

The key employee is (name), who founded the business, owns the business and has the title of... (Name) has worked in this industry for ... years at a variety of companies. (Name) is particularly strong in the areas of (management, product development, servicing customers, finance, accounting, engineering, marketing, sales, etc.) At (previous company #1) he/she had experience in ... At (previous company #2) he/she had experience in... Areas that (name) is weaker in are ... In these areas assistance will be provided by (an outside accounting firm, an outside law firm, consultants, part-time employees, a new hire).

Three key employees

The company has three employees who can considered to be key. (Name) is responsible for management, finances, accounting and other administration issues. (He or she) has previously held the following relevant positions... (Name) will be responsible for (products or services). (He or she) has previously held the following relevant positions... (Name) will be responsible for sales, marketing, and customer relations. (He or she) has previously held the following relevant positions... [*See Business Plan Example #33*]

President/CEO: Existing Business

(Name) is the President and principal shareholder of the company. (He/she) has (# of) years experience in the (relevant field) industry, and was (Job Title) for (Previous Employer) where he gained valuable experience in (functional area). He formed (Company Name) in (Year), and the company has had an average annual growth rate of ...% over the past ...years, attributable to (reason for growth) and the excellent management team the President has put in place. (Name) owns ...% of the stock in (Company Name) and acts as (Board Position Title) of the Board of Directors.

President/CEO: New Business

The principal owner, (Name), has been involved in the (name of industry) industry since (Year). He/she attended (College), and studied (Major), and then attended (Graduate School), where he received a (Advanced Degree) degree in (discipline) in (Year). In (Year), he began working for (previous employer) as a (position). (Name)'s expertise is focused in the area of (area of expertise), which is central to the operations of the proposed business. He has an excellent reputation throughout the industry and brings tremendous strength and experience to the new enterprise.

Lawn Masters of Newton

Business Plan Example #33

Key Personnel

The company has three employees who can considered to be key. Jack Duffy, President and CEO, is responsible for management, finances, accounting and other administration issues. He has been with Lawn Masters of Newton for over ten years, and previously held the position of Regional Manager for Home Depot in New England. Ed Davis, Vice President, will be responsible for services and overall operations, including training and supervision of all the work crews. He has been with Lawn Masters of Newton for five years, and has a degree in environmental studies from the University of Massachusetts. Janice Kendall will be responsible for sales, marketing and customer relations. She is new to our company, and was most recently an Assistant Director for Publicity with the Mass. Audubon Society.

The compensation and incentives plan offered to key personnel is designed to give these individuals a significant stake in the company's success as a way of encouraging top performance and of retaining them in their positions. In addition to salaries, compensation for key personnel will include profit sharing (set at 10% of pre-tax earnings) and bonuses based on newly registered accounts.

Board of Directors
Members of the Board of Directors have been selected for their ability to bring specialized skills and experience to the company. In addition to the three principals involved in daily operations, these Directors will include Frank White, whose expertise lies in the area of small business law, Stan Novak, who works extensively with several community organizations in Newton in a fund-raising capacity, and Bill Miles, who is the Chairman of the Newton Community Gardeners organization. These non-management Directors will not be compensated for their participation.

Chief Financial Officer

(Name) has had a lengthy and broad background in financial management. After receiving an MBA from (Business School) in (Year), (Name) served as (Title) for (previous employer) for (#) years, as (Title) for (previous employer) for (#) years, and as (Title) for (previous employer) for (#) years. As CFO, (he/she) will oversee the entire Finance Department for (company name) and be responsible for all of its operations.

Vice President, Sales & Marketing

(Name) will have primary responsibility for the company's sales and marketing activities, including management of the field sales organization and the customer service department. (He/she) has an extensive background in all aspects of sales and marketing management, with (#) years with (previous employer) as (job title) and (#) years with (previous employer) as (job title). This much relevant experience in the (relevant field) industry insures his/her will perform well in this position.

Vice President, Production

(Name)'s (#) years of direct experience in operations and production management in the (relevant industry) field is a tremendous asset to this company. (He/she) is thoroughly familiar with all aspects of the production process, from the start-up and bidding phases through completion. In (his/her) past positions with (previous employer) and (previous employers), (Name) was also able to develop new and improved processes in the area of customer service and customer satisfaction.

Vice President, Human Resources

(Name) began (his/her) career in human resources in (Year) with (previous employer), where (he/she) was involved in incentive and employee benefit plans and the development of equal opportunity/diversity programs. In our organization, (he/she) will handle a similarly wide range of HR functions, as well as employee recruitment and hiring.

Management Compensation and Incentives

The compensation and incentive plan offered to key personnel is designed to give these individuals a significant stake in the company's success as a way of encouraging top performance and retaining them in their positions. In addition to salaries, compensation for key personnel will include (stock options, profit sharing set at ...% of pre-tax earnings, bonuses based on ...) [*See Business Plan Example #33*]

Board of Directors

Members of the Board of Directors have been selected for their ability to bring specialized skills and experience to the company. In addition to the (# of) principals involved in daily operations, these Directors will include (Name), whose expertise lies in the area of (area of expertise), (Name), who will be counted on for (area of expertise), and (Name), who is extremely knowledgeable in the area of (area of expertise). These non-management Directors (will/will not) be compensated for their participation at a per diem rate ($ daily rate). [*See Business Plan Example #33*]

Organizational structure

This section explains the reporting structure in your firm and how work is divided between different people. If you have a formal organization chart, you should include the chart at the end of the business plan. For a very small business with a half-dozen or fewer employees (or for a less complex business plan) you may prefer to skip this section and include relevant information when discussing key personnel.

Select and edit all that apply...

Basic organizational structure statement

The company is divided into ...(departments, work groups, units, divisions, informal areas of focus). These are the key areas and their respective responsibilities... (Note if an organizational chart is included at the end of the business plan.)

Overview of the organizational structure

1. Executive. Consisting of the President, (name), and ...support staff. Responsibilities include overall management, determining strategic direction and...

2. Finance/Accounting. Headed by the (CFO, Vice President of Finance, Controller, Accounting Manager) and consisting of ...employees. Responsibilities include producing monthly financial statements, preparing cash flow forecasts, handling day-to-day banking relations, credit, collections, and...

3. Sales/Marketing. Headed by the (Vice President of Marketing, The Marketing Manager, the Sales Manager) and consisting of...employees. Responsibilities include developing marketing strategy, developing advertising concepts, arranging for product and placement of advertising, arranging for publicity, directly selling to key accounts, management of independent commission sales reps who sell to smaller accounts, management of relationships with distributors.

4. (Manufacturing or Service). Headed by the (Vice President of Manufacturing, Vice President of Service, the Plant Manager, the Service Manager) and consisting of...employees. Responsible for (manufacturing products or delivering services) including...

5. (Include other distinctive areas your company may have such as Engineering, Customer Service or Support, Human Resources, Operations, Shipping & Receiving, etc.)

Informal organizational structure

Our organizational structure is very informal, without written job descriptions of specific departments formally dividing responsibilities. This is partially because there are so few employees, partially because we are all willing to pitch in to do whatever it takes to get the job done, and partially because we sometimes are forced to shift all of our focus to work together on the most pressing priorities. As a matter of practice however, here is who takes the primary role in each of the major functional areas:

Finance: (name).

Marketing and Sales: (name).

Operations/Office: (name).

(Product or Service): (name). [*See Business Plan Example #34*]

Reliance on outside resources

Being a very small company with only ...employees, our selection and use of outside contractors and service providers is an important part of our operation. Here is a break-out of the key outsiders that will be supporting our business:

Accounting: (firm or individual) (responsibilities)

Legal: (firm or individual) (responsibilities)

Other: (name if available) (responsibilities)

[*See Business Plan Example #34*]

Planned change in organizational structure

Until now our organization has been divided into ...groups: (list each group). We intend to reorganize into...groups (list groups). Essentially the (group to change) will be (eliminated, merged into the...group, broken into ...new group and the...new group). Accompanying this change we will be (hiring a new manager, hiring new...people, eliminating...positions). We are making this change because... [*See Business Plan Example #34*]

Lawn Masters of Newton

Business Plan Example #34

Organizational structure

Our organizational structure is very informal, without written descriptions of specific areas of responsibilities. This is primarily because the three key members of the management team work very closely across many aspects of the company's operations. As a matter of practice however, here is who takes the primary role in each of the major functional areas:

Finance: Jack Duffy
Marketing and Sales: Janice Kendall
Operations/Office: Ed Davis

Being a very small company, our selection and use of outside contractors and service providers is an important part of our operation. Here is a break-out of the key outsiders that will be supporting our business:

Accounting: Arnold Financial Services, taxes and strategic planning
Legal: White & Associates, review and prepare legal documents
Graphics & Design: Desktop Graphics Inc., brochures and other collateral

---

Human resources plan

It would be appropriate to discuss here specific issues such as which positions need to be created and filled, your procedures for hiring employees, your policies on reviewing employees, salary and benefit policies, and training plans.. You could also discuss your overall strategy for human resources, explain the kind of company culture you want to foster, present your philosophy about human resources, or describe how your human resources approach will be different than that of other firms.

Select and edit all that apply...

Basic human resources statement

We recognize that human resources are an extremely important asset. Hence we will screen new applicants very carefully including in-person interviews and reference checks. We will review each employee's performance regularly, and when possible promote from within. Our salaries and benefit packages will be competitive with those offered by other firms in our area. [*See Business Plan Example #35*]

Lawn Masters of Newton

Business Plan Example #35

Human Resources Plan

We recognize that human resources are an extremely important asset, especially in a service business in which work is performed on customer's property. Our competitors do not generally recognize this fact, and in general, the personnel standards in the lawn maintenance industry are very low. Often, unskilled, unqualified individuals are hired, paid minimum wage, and worked hard until they leave. Field staff of this sort obviously do not reflect well on the company.

At Lawn Masters of Newton, we have decided that although all of our field staff are seasonal workers, we will nevertheless hire only people who are qualified or who can be trained to do the work as required, and who can interact with customers in a friendly and professional manner. Thus, we screen new applicants very carefully, including in-person interviews and reference checks. We will strive to hire people who have a solid work ethic and work well with others. Working well with others is especially important in our system of 3-person work crews, each having a consistent set of scheduled assignments and a crew leader.

We will recruit employees by newspaper help-wanted advertising, and offering referral bonuses to current employees. We will review each employee's performance regularly, and when possible promote from within.

The company's salary structure will be higher than market rates, and an extremely competitive benefit package will be offered (most of our competitors offer no benefits at all to seasonal workers) not only to help the recruitment effort, but to increase the chance of retaining employees for the entire lawn maintenance season and hopefully bringing them back next year. Benefits offered will include paid vacation days after the season (accrued at a rate of 1.25 days/month of employment), and a comprehensive health plan (employer pays 50%).

Training

Building a sense of teamwork among all personnel is an essential component for the success of the business. By allocating significant time and resources to staff training, we expect to increase every employee's ability to provide valuable services for our customers, and to feel that he or she is an important, contributing part of the organization. Responsibility for training will come under Operations (Ed Davis), but all three members of the management team have taken part in developing or reviewing training materials or in actually delivering training sessions as appropriate.

Due to the short, seasonal nature of the business, all employees need feedback on their performance with a much greater frequency than the normal annual review process. Lawn Masters of Newton uses a standard form, completed on a weekly basis by the crew leader. This form contains specific feedback on job performance, and also makes summary recommendations as to areas for improvement.

Human resources strategy statement

Our human resources strategy will be (to treat all employees with respect, to create a high performance environment, to create a positive and productive environment, to be fair and consistent, to empower employees, to involve employees in decision-making as much as possible, to keep our labor costs low). Important elements of this strategy are...

Staffing Plan: New Business

New staff will be added as the company achieves predetermined revenue benchmarks. As reflected in the financials, the total number of staff positions will reach (#) by the end of year one, (# of) by the end of year two, and (# of) by the end of year three. Our recruitment strategies for identifying candidates and hiring individuals to fill these positions will be based on a combination of referrals, classified advertising in local newspapers, and (other strategies). When new hires are accomplished, subsequent orientation and training will be the responsibility of (position title).

Support Staff: New Business

A total of (# of) support personnel will be hired within the first (# of) months to accomplish on-going operational functions such as (job function), (job function), and (job function). Specific positions to be filled in this initial period are:

_____   _____-time $_____ per hour

_____   _____-time $_____ per hour

_____   _____-time $_____ per hour

Hiring strategy

We will strive to hire people who (are flexible and creative, have a solid work ethic, are willing to work hard, work well with others, have excellent references, have a record of high performance, a good ability to get along with others, an ability to work with a diverse group of people, work well in a team environment). We will recruit employees by (newspaper help-wanted advertising, advertising on the internet, searching resume databases, using employment agencies, offering referral bonuses to current employees). For most positions we will (do initial screening by telephone, conduct in-person interviews, have candidates fill out an application form, get references from previous employers or schools, do extensive background checks). [*See Business Plan Example #35*]

Salaries and benefits statement

In setting salaries we will (examine each situation individually, follow a company-wide job grading system, be consistent for comparable positions throughout the organization, match industry standards, aim to set salaries ...% above the average in our area, above the average in our industry). Our benefits policies will include (profit-sharing, bonuses, cash rewards, stock options, paid holidays, paid vacations, personal time, medical insurance, an HMO plan, dental insurance, eye glasses insurance, life insurance, short-term disability insurance, long-term disability insurance, educational assistance).

Salary and Benefits Higher than Market

The company's salary structure will be slightly higher than market rates, and an extremely competitive benefit package will be offered not only to help the recruitment effort, but to increase the chance of retaining employees and maintaining an experienced staff. Benefits offered will include (# of) weeks of paid vacation, a comprehensive health (and dental) plan, (benefit), and (benefit). [*See Business Plan Example #35*]

Outside contractors, freelancers

To obtain specialized expertise the company (will, has) engaged the services of outside contractors and freelancers. Here are people that have been lined up to date:

(Function)   (Person)
(Function)   (Person)
(Function)   (Person)

Recruitment: New Business

Several approaches will be utilized in parallel in order to recruit the new staff members who will be needed as the company grows, including classified newspaper advertising, a paid incentive referral program for current employees, and (recruitment strategy). Candidates will undergo a thorough interview process with at least (# of) current employees on separate occasions. Wherever possible, competency tests will be administered as a part of the selection process.

Staff Development: New Business

In addition to the key personnel, other necessary functions will be accomplished through a combination of new hires (full- and part-time) and independent contractors. In specific, the following new employees are anticipated:

# Positions	Position Title	Expected Time to Hire

The following functions will be handled through contractors:

# Positions	Function	Expected Time to Hire

Training

Building a sense of teamwork among all personnel is an essential component for the success of the business. By allocating significant time and resources to staff training, we expect to increase every employee's ability to create positive change in the workplace and to help everyone feel that he or she is an important, contributing part of the organization. Responsibility for training will come under Human Resources, but key managers from every department will take part in developing or reviewing training materials or in actually delivering training sessions as appropriate. Also included in the budget projections are funds for bringing in outside consultants for staff training purposes as needed. [*See Business Plan Example #35*]

Improve employee capabilities

We believe that our employees are truly one of our most important assets. We intend to further invest in their capabilities and job satisfaction by offering the following programs (full or partial tuition reimbursement, out of house seminars, in house seminars, an informal series of seminars by experts on our staff, reimbursement for professionally related books, an in-house book library, an audio cassette library, a video library, a multi-media training center). Employee capabilities we are particularly interested in improving are...

Performance Reviews

All employees will have an annual performance review conducted by the manager to whom they directly report. All managers will complete a standard form and meet with each staff member individually to discuss it. This form will contain specific feedback on job performance, and will also make summary recommendations as to areas for improvement and (salary increases/bonuses).

To increase morale

To increase company morale we plan on taking a number of steps. We will (rotate people among jobs, give more emphasis to promotion from within, hold regular company parties, have regular company luncheons, start an employee reward program, be more responsive to employee's concerns, give out gifts adorned with the company logo, redecorate employee work areas, give all-employee briefings on the progress of the company, make an effort to publicly praise notable accomplishments by employees at all levels, increase the interaction between different departments, celebrate company milestones).

Improve a particular function

We will improve the quality of our (function or department). We will hire a new, experienced person to revamp this department. We will set new standards of expectations for this area. We will carefully review the performance of each person in the department. And we will carefully monitor the department as a whole.

Lower employee turnover

We will decrease employee turnover to less than ...% per year, by (increasing the frequency of employee reviews, revamping our benefits program, by making our wages more competitive, starting an employee bonus program, hiring a human resources manager, holding exit interviews to identify and reduce the reasons that employees are leaving).

Product/service delivery

There are many different ways in which you can approach the discussion of product or service delivery. One approach is to emphasize the steps that you will take to insure that your product or service delivery supports either your business strategy or your product or service positioning strategy. Another approach is to simply summarize how you plan on producing products or delivering services. Still another approach may be to discuss standards you will use.

Select and edit all that apply...

Basic product/service delivery statement
We intend that our (product or service) delivery will support our positioning plan for our (product or service) which is to (identify positioning strategy as described in earlier parts of this business plan.) To meet this objective we will...

Description of product development approach
Before giving the go ahead on a new product we will (get customer feedback, do market surveys, do a feasibility study, do a focus group, research comparative offerings). The decision to proceed will be largely based on an the following factors... The actual (design, engineering, development) of the product will be done by... The following manufacture will be done (by a contract manufacturer, at our facility at, by arrangement with, at...company).

Description of service standards approach
These are some of the standards we will use to help insure that we provide high quality service:
1. We will answer our phones within 3 rings.
2. We will provide a free, written estimate within 72 hours.
3. We will begin work within 7 days of receiving a signed agreement.
4. We will not interrupt work for any reason until we finish a job.
5. We will use the highest quality materials available.
6. We will leave the work area clean and neat at the end of each day.
7. We will follow-up after every job to be sure the customer is satisfied.
8. We will guarantee satisfaction for all of our work.
[*See Business Plan Example #36*]

Controlling costs
We will control costs by (keeping our labor costs low, getting competitive bids on major purchases, arranging for a long-term delivery contract, using just-in-time inventory methods, watching overhead costs closely, checking variances with budget each month, offering employee's awards for cost-saving ideas, instituting a gain-sharing program, benchmarking all costs with industry standards.)

Quality control
We will insure that our quality is high by (having a specific quality control program, having specific standards that must be adhered to, doing spot checks, selecting high quality vendors, double-checking crucial steps, having a rigorous hiring process, appointing a quality control manager, having ... personally inspect each job, communicating to all employees that quality is our first priority, benchmark our offerings with those of competitors, conducting customer surveys, making follow-up calls after each assignment).

State of the art focused

Supporting our strategic goal of being on the cutting edge in new product development is a multi-faceted process. To keep our employees up to speed with the latest developments we will (attend seminars, attend trade conferences, meet regularly with outside experts, maintain close relations with universities, subscribe to the appropriate journals, have outside experts give in-house presentations, hire expert consultants, obtain research information from other firms, pursue a joint development project with..., enter licensing agreements).

Delivering quality, personalized service

In order to deliver high quality, personalized service we will (carefully select all employees, put each employee through a careful training process, make sure each employee understands our way of delivering quality service to each customer, have immediate back-up support available for more difficult service issues, give employees enough latitude so that they can respond immediately to almost all customer requests, base employee compensation largely upon customer satisfaction). [*See Business Plan Example #36*]

Lawn Masters of Newton

Business Plan Example #36

Service delivery

Here are some of the standards we have adopted to help insure that we provide high quality service:

1. We will answer our phones within 3 rings.
2. We will provide a free, written estimate within 48 hours.
3. We will begin work within 3 days of receiving a signed agreement.
4. We will not interrupt work for any reason until we finish a job.
5. We will use the highest quality equipment and supplies available.
6. We will leave the property clean and neat at the end of each day.
7. We will follow-up after every job to be sure the customer is satisfied.
8. We will guarantee satisfaction for all of our work.

Our strategy is built around offering highly personalized service to our customers. Integral to this approach is the careful selection of field staff, in-depth training so that they may respond quickly to customer requests, and in-depth back-up support for more difficult requests.

Quality control changes
Overall responsibility for control is handled by Ed Davis. After a major review of our current procedures, which included soliciting input from customers, we have redesigned certain aspects of the process. In particular, we will institute new incentive programs and emphasize training and rewards to help motivate employees to ensure that our high quality standards are being met.

Using computers to cut inventory needs

We will use our computer and software systems to closely monitor inventory requirements. This will allow us to effectively operate with much lower levels of inventory that has been the case in the past--without increasing the risk of stock outs.

Selecting suppliers not just on price

In the past we have largely selected suppliers on the basis of price. This has produced several problems which we would like to avoid in the future. So now we are using additional criteria for choosing suppliers and assigning outside work. For work involving a cost greater than $..., we are adding the following criteria for the selection of suppliers... For suppliers under a cost of $...the additional criteria will be limited to...

Relationships with suppliers

We believe that maintaining excellent relationships with our suppliers is an important part of successfully delivering our (products or services). We pay our suppliers within terms; we treat their sales people and customer service people with respect; we maintain a relationship with key executives at our core suppliers; and we let our suppliers know that we appreciate their work. Because of these steps, our suppliers are willing to really go to bat for us when we need their extra help. This is particularly important when (specifications must be changed at the last minutes, we have a rush job, when schedules must be re-arranged, when we want to meet the needs of a particularly demanding customer, etc.)

Order turnaround

We will have an order turnaround from receipt of order to the time it leaves our warehouse of no greater than ... To do this we will take the following steps...

Customer service/support

Customer service is an increasingly important aspect of running a successful business. Some organizations make it a centerpiece of their marketing campaigns. Will you handle all aspects of customer service in-house, or will you outsource some of it, to a fulfillment service, for example? If you intend to pay significant attention to customer service, describe how you will do it. Will it be a part of on-going training programs? Will you devise special employee incentives? Will you make an effort to solicit feedback from the customers, and if so, how?

Select and edit all that apply...

Basic customer/service support statement

Customer service/support will be handled by... During our normal business hours calls will be handled by the (position). During non business hours calls will be taken by... Since customer service/support is an integral part of our business, we will strive to keep our customers satisfied at all times. We will give particular effort to...

Improve customer service

We seek to improve our customer service by taking the following steps: (decrease waiting time at our peak service periods, adding some support capability to our World Wide Web site, offering support by e-mail, offering support by fax, offering a fax-back program, expanding our phone capacity, installing a voice mail system, increasing our hours, out-sourcing our service, monitoring occasional service calls, seeking customer input, installing toll free customer service lines).

Customer service plan: new business

We intend to prioritize customer service and make it a key component of our marketing programs. We believe that providing our customers with what they want, when and how they want it, is the key to repeat business and to word-of-mouth advertising. Not only will we train our employees to deliver excellent service, we will give them the flexibility to respond creatively to client requests. In addition, we will continually monitor our clients' level of satisfaction with our service through surveys and other convenient feedback opportunities. [*See Business Plan Example #37*]

Fulfillment: existing business

The new internal information systems to be deployed will have an extremely positive impact on the order fulfillment process. In the past, too much time was wasted in an ineffi-cient order communication process. Now, we expect to reduce order processing time by (amount of time), which will result in faster shipping and higher levels of customer satisfac-tion. [*See Business Plan Example #37*]

Customer service: existing business

We have discovered that our customer service standards have not kept pace with the levels of service now offered by some of our competitors. Therefore we have designed an exten-sive employee training program, involving everyone from (position title) to (position title), with the goal of (measurable goal).

Customer service: new business

An important part of our operating plan is to make contact with customers after the sale/services are rendered. We believe that new sources of revenue can be developed through additional post-sale services, and that our client base can be more effectively retained through this approach.

Customer service: shipping

Our relatively high cost of shipping has put us at a competitive disadvantage. The current cost of shipping for an average order is $..., which we feel can be reduced by ...%. We intend to achieve this cost reduction by putting our overall shipping requirements out to bid.

Lawn Masters of Newton

Business Plan Example #37

Customer service/support

We intend to prioritize customer service and make it a key component of our marketing programs. We believe that providing our customers with what they want in the area of lawn maintenance, when and how they want it is the key to repeat business and to word-of-mouth advertising. Not only will we train our employees to deliver excellent service, we will give them the flexibility to respond creatively to client requests. In addition, we will continually monitor our clients' level of satisfaction with our service through surveys and convenient feedback opportunities.

We plan on using the World Wide Web for a significant portion of our service/support effort. On the web we can offer support 24 hours a day, 365 days a year. And on the web, customers don't have to wait for the next available service representative. Once the service area of our web site is up the cost to maintain it will be minimal. On our web site we plan on offering a choice of text options explaining basic service issues, lists of frequently asked questions and answers about lawn maintenance, and the ability to e-mail for help with highly specific questions and any requested changes in the scheduled maintenance plan.

Using the world wide web

We plan on using the World Wide Web for a significant portion of our service/support effort. On the web we can offer support 24 hours a day, 365 days a year. And on the Web, customers don't have to wait for the next available service representative. Once the service area of our Web site is up, the cost to maintain it will be minimal. On our Web site we plan on offering (a choice of text options explaining basic service issues, lists of other resources for help, lists of frequently asked questions and answers, a extensive searchable database of service/support information, the ability to e-mail for help with highly specific questions, current postings of newly discovered service issues). [*See Business Plan Example #37*]

Order turn-around

We shall turn around all orders in a maximum of... by... In order to accomplish this we will need to...

Decrease service call time

We will decrease the time spent of the average service call by about ... We will accomplish this by...

Response to service calls

We shall generally respond to service calls within... Even during busier periods we intend to respond no later than... Emergency or high priority calls we intend to respond to within...

Decrease waiting time

We intend to decrease our average waiting time for (incoming calls, service calls, support calls, our customers). We hope to decrease our response time from typically... to ... by (date).

Facilities

Your location and the facility itself may be an important aspect of your company's image. Describe the advantages and disadvantages of the location. What kind of a facility is it? Will clients be coming there? What kind of equipment will be there, and how will it be furnished. Be sure that you take future growth into account. For how long will this facility be adequate?

Select and edit all that apply...

Basic facilities statement: existing business

The company currently (owns/leases) (# of) square feet of space located at (address/city,state). This space is used as the primary production facility as well as the main office and administrative headquarters. The total number of full- or part-time employees working in this facility is (#), for a square footage per person of (#). This facility will continue to meet all of our needs during the remaining period of the current lease, which ends in (date). There is an option to renew at the end of this period, which we expect to do. If more space is needed then, additional space is expected to be available nearby at approximately the same price per square foot.

Basic facilities statement: new business

As a service business, the location of our facility and the professional image it presents are essential parts of our marketing strategy. Since our target market is (target market), we feel that our company needs to be located near other businesses that serve a similar demographic profile, preferably with parking and public transportation facilities nearby. Rental fees in the range of ($) to ($) is another important factor. In the city of (location), satisfying these criteria means one of the following areas or neighborhoods: (neighborhood), (neighborhood), or (neighborhood).

Home Office

This business will be operated out of a home office, primarily in order to reduce expenditures. The space to be utilized for this purpose is (# of) square feet, which is perfectly adequate for the foreseeable future. The area is zoned for business, and the space features a separate entrance. As a (type of business), all of the client meetings will take place offsite, at the client's office. The home office will be appropriate for other business meetings, such as meetings with vendors and contractors.

Retail

Our major factors in site selection consist of traffic flow, parking, median income of the area, and rental costs. The location we have chosen, (address, city/town), meets or exceeds our parameters for all of the criteria. With the presence of (other retailer) and (other retailer) in the immediate vicinity, the traffic level is already high, over (# of) cars per day, but not higher than the existing roadways can handle smoothly. The location is very accessible, and there is ample parking available. According to the most recent US Census data, the median household income for the relevant Standard Metropolitan Statistical Area (SMSA) is also very attractive – over $... per year. The rent, $... per square foot, is at the high end of our acceptable range, but still falls within our target parameters.

Equipment

A limited amount of specialized equipment is utilized at the facility to (to test, manufacture, design, package, etc.). including (equipment #1), (equipment #2), and (equipment #3). Approximately (# of) square feet is required for this operation. In addition to this production equipment, there are over (# of) computers in use for applications ranging from order entry and inventory control to word processing and graphics. Office equipment present at the facility includes (# of) copy machines, (# of) scanners, and (# of) printers.

Furnishings and Fixtures

We will be renting an unfurnished facility, and will need to acquire furniture which will create a professional look and a contemporary feel, since clients will be coming to the office on a regular basis. In order to reduce initial expenditures, we plan to lease these furnishings, which will include desks, chairs, lighting, cabinets, framed works of modern art, potted plants, and a sofa and easy chairs for the waiting area.

Relocation

Our market research shows that the current location of our facility, (address, city or town), is one of the primary factors holding back our revenue growth. The basic problem with the location is (current problem). After considering several options to address this problem, we have decided to relocate to a new facility at (address, city or town). This new space offers a number of significant advantages over our current location, including (advantages).

Expansion

The company's current facility is not large enough to accommodate the new size and scope of the business. We are utilizing (# of) square feet at the present time, and plan to move to a new facility offering at least (# of) square feet, which meets current and anticipated needs for the foreseeable future. [*See Business Plan Example #38*]

Increase capacity of facilities

We will increase the capacity of our (plant, warehouse, office, etc.) We will accomplish this by (using a more efficient floor plan, by using shared offices, by building an addition, by leasing additional space, by moving to a new location).

Increase utilization of facilities

We will improve the utilization of our (plant, warehouse, offices, facility, building). We will re-organize the layout to be more efficient, and to be a more effective place to work. We will do this by...

New facilities: existing business

Continued growth of our business demands that we increase the number of locations. Our current facilities are located in (location). Based on research into our current customer base and other parts of the greater metropolitan area with a similar demographic profile, we are planning to open satellite offices in (area) in (month, year) and (area) in (month, year).

Facility improvements

We plan on making improvements to our current facility in order to (improve our capacity, to accommodate more employees, to make for a more efficient work flow, to make for a more attractive work environment, to make the work environment more consistent with our business image). These are the specific steps we plan on taking...

Create a more professional work environment

We will create a more professional work environment. To do this we will (improve the landscaping, clean up the grounds, get new company signs, improve the entrance way, get a new receptionist work station, get new furniture, repaint the walls, buy new or used office cubicles, carpet the floors, encourage everyone to clean up their work area, set up a conference room).

Upgrade equipment

We intend to upgrade the following office equipment: (personal computers, servers, computer printers, phone system, voice mail, copiers, fax machines, postage meters, shipping equipment).

Automate functions

We will automate the following function(s)... We will achieve this by...

Enhance web site

We will expand the capability of our Web site to include (customer support, job postings, product information, complete product catalog, news releases, internal news letters, etc.).

Paperless office

We will move to a virtually paperless office by (enter date). To do this we will need the following additional equipment...

REMAINING COMPLETE BUSINESS PLAN COMPONENTS

To further assist you in assembling your business plan we have included three sections to use as a reference. We have provided five sample business plans, a section called Workshops and Q&A, all of these are designed to guide you to a business plan that will help you achieve your goals, whatever they are.

Sample Plans

The five sample plans provided are as follows:

1. Rainbow Kites, Inc.
2. Lawn Masters of Newton
3. Internet Service Provider
4. Consulting Services
5. Chinese Restaurant

The first two plans on the list were created using this product and should give you an accurate idea of what this software is capable of. The final three are plans from actual businesses provided by consultants. Again these should give a good example of how a business plan should be assembled.

Workshops

There are four video workshops included in Complete Business Plan. Each has been written and taped by Bob Adams, the author of this program. Each section is designed to put you in a "face-to-face" meeting with Bob and ask him for "Streetwise Advice" on different aspects of business plans. If you choose not to view the videos or are using the Lite version you may read Bob's advice in text format.

The four workshops provided in this software are:

1. Creating Your Business Plan
2. Getting a Bank Loan
3. Attracting Equity Investors
4. Planning for Profits

Q&A's

Q&A's are just what the title of this section suggests, answers to some of the most commonly asked questions to business planning questions. These are ideal for those looking for both reassurance and basic guidance on running and planning a business. The eight topics covered in this section are:

1. Business Ideas
2. Preparing the Plan
3. Getting Equity Money
4. Annual Planning
5. Using the Business Plan
6. Strategy
7. Franchising
8. Buying a Business

IMPROVING SYSTEM PERFORMANCE

Some commonly asked questions about improving system performance with our product are answered below. For specific trouble-shooting information about a section of the program, check in the on-line help file, this manual, and on our web site - www.adamsmedia.com. If these do not answer your questions, contact technical support.

Note that the instructions for Windows 95/98 and Windows NT4.0 are different than earlier versions of Windows and Windows NT.

Windows 95/98 and Windows NT 4.0

Q. I keep getting a print buffer overload message when I print the spreadsheets. What can I do?

A. Note that these spreadsheets contain a huge amount of information in comparison to most items that you print. Printing an entire workbook may simply overwhelm your printer.

To troubleshoot this problem, print out the spreadsheets individually. Be patient when doing this - even printing a single spreadsheet may take a while.

If this does not work, try following these steps.

1) Go to your My Computer icon and double-click.
2) Double-click on the Printer icon
3) Highlight the printer you are using and go under the File menu and choose Properties.
4) Click on the Details Tab.
5) Hit the button for Spool Settings
6) Write down you current setting for spool data format.
7) Check off Print directly to Printer.
8) Close all the dialog boxes you have opened and re-start our program.

If you try printing now, it should work, though it may be slow. If this does not work, please contact technical support.

To restore your former printer settings, follow the steps above, but choose Spool printer jobs so printing finishes faster and restore your spool data format to what you wrote down above.

Q. I get an error message telling me that my computer is operating in large fonts mode and to switch to small fonts, how do I do this?

A. In Windows 95 go to Start and Choose Settings, then Control Panel. Double click the Display icon. Click on the Settings tab. Toward the bottom of the screen you will see "Font Size" select "small fonts" from the drop-down menu and click on Apply.

For Windows 98 follow the above until you get to the Settings tab. Click on the "Advanced" button. The top of the screen will say "Font Size." Select Small Fonts from the drop-down menu and click on Apply.

Q. Will a screen saver interfere with the videos in Adams Streetwise Business Plans?

A. In general, no, provided the delay for the screen saver turning on is set higher than the length of the longest video in the product - approximately 3 minutes.

However, to insure that no interference occurs, you can turn off your screen savers by doing the following.

1) Right click on the Windows Desktop and choose Properties.
2) Click on the tab that says Screen Saver in the Display Properties dialog box. In the list of screensavers which appears in this window, scroll up to None and choose it.
3) Hit Ok and your screen savers will be turned off.

Q. How can I improve overall performance of the Adams Streetwise Business Plan.? (Windows 95 only)

A. A computer works most efficiently when you perform periodic system maintenance. Run the Scandisk program in the Accessories listing in the Programs menu. Also run Disk Defragmenter from that same menu.

Q. How can I optimize CD-ROM performance?

A. Windows 95 and Windows NT generally handle most performance issues for CD-ROM performance automatically. If you suspect there is a problem, you can go into your Control Panel, double-click on the System icon, choose the Performance tab, hit File system, and choose the CD-ROM tab. Make sure that the Optimize Access pattern is set correctly for your speed CD-ROM. If you suspect it not, contact your system manufacturer or consult your system documentation to see if there is a reason for the current setting. Change it if appropriate.

you can also change the Supplemental Cache size. Again, consult your system documentation or your hardware vendor or manufacturer for information on the appropriate settings for your CD-ROM drive. A large cache size does not always result in an increase in system performance.

Q. How can I improve the graphics for the Adams Complete Business Plan if they look grainy and small?

A. This will usually only occur if you have display properties set up to display only sixteen colors. To check this, right click on your Desktop and choose properties. In the dialog box that comes up, choose settings. If the color palette setting says 16 colors (not High Color - 16Bit), consult with your system documentation to ascertain whether or not your video card and/or monitor can support a higher setting. If so change this setting to 256 colors or higher and re-boot your computer as instructed. You should only do this if you are certain your computer will support these settings. If your unsure contact your hardware vendor.

If the choice for color palette does not allow you to choose anything but 16 colors, you are using a VGA video driver. In most situations, you will find your computer is capable of supporting other video drivers with additional color options. For information on installing other drivers, consult your system or video card documentation or contact your hardware vendor.

Q. I hear no sound when using the CD-ROM version of the Adams Streetwise Complete Business Plan?

A. If you have no sound in other applications, you have a larger system problem which you need to contact your hardware vendor about. Before you do so, make sure to check all your speaker connections, the volume settings on your computer, and your sound card documentation for troubleshooting options.

If our application is the only one not generating sound, contact technical support..

Note that if you can hear music from an audio CD, this does not mean your sound card is functioning correctly. Check you sound card by trying to play a sound file on your computer, not an audio CD.

Q. Why does the right side scroll bar disappear sometimes when I move between spreadsheet?

A. Sometimes, because of the amount of memory needed to run the complex formulas in the spreadsheets you may switch too quickly. This may also happen when you open a new spreadsheet before the computer has finished with your last task. To correct this move to another speadsheet and then after a slight puase return to the speadsheet you wish to work on.

Windows for Workgroups 3.11, Windows 3.1, and Windows NT 3.51

Q. Adams Streetwise Complete Business Plan seems to be running very slowly on my computer. How can I improve performance?

A. In Windows 3.1 and Windows 3.11, you should run scandisk and Defrag. Do not do this in Windows NT. Quit Windows and Go to a DOS prompt. Type Scandisk at the prompt and follow the on screen instructions to check your hard drive for errors. After you have run Scandisk and returned to a DOS prompt, type Defrag and follow the on screen instructions to optimize your hard drive's performance. If you have any questions about either of these questions, consult your DOS user's manual.

Note that before proceeding with Defrag, you should back up crucial files on your hard drive.

Q. I have tried all of the above to improve system performance. What else can I do?

A. There are several options

1) Add more RAM. You will notice improved performance from even an additional 4 MB of RAM. Adding more RAM will give our program more room to move large video and spreadsheet files, which are memory intensive, into RAM.

2) Free up additional hard disk space. If you can keep 10 to 15 MB free, our program will function much better

3) Additional free hard drive space can work with the virtual memory settings of your computer. For best results, use a permanent swap file setting of at least 5 MB. You can change your swap file settings by opening up the main Window in Program Manger, opening your Control Panel, then the 386 Enhanced control. Double-click on the virtual memory buttons to make changes.

Q. I hear no sound when using the CD-ROM version of the Adams Streetwise Complete Business Plan?

A. If you have no sound in other applications, you have a larger system problem which you need to contact your hardware vendor about. Before you do so, make sure to check all your speaker connections, the volume settings ion your computer, and your sound card documentation for troubleshooting options.

   If our application is the only one not generating sound, contact technical support..

   Note that if you can hear music from an audio CD, this does not mean your sound card is functioning correctly. Check you sound card by trying to play a sound file on your computer, not an audio CD.

Q. How can I improve the graphics for the Adams Complete Business Plan if they look grainy and small?

A. This will usually only occur if you have display properties set up to display to VGA, 16 colors .To check this, open the main window and open Windows Setup. If the listing says VGA, consult with your system documentation to ascertain whether or not your video card and/or monitor can support a different video driver with 256 colors. Follow the instructions in the system documentation to change the driver. You can follow the instructions below to install a 256 color SVGA driver if one comes with your system setup, however this should only be done if you can be sure your system supports it. If your unsure contact your hardware vendor.

1) In the Windows Set Up window, choose change systems settings.

2) In the Window that comes up, scroll through the list under display looking for an SVGA 640x480 small fonts video driver with 256 color. Choose it and hit OK. If you do not have this video driver, you can try any of the following:

   VGA - 256 color
   SVGA -256 color 800x600 small font
   SVGA -256 color 800x600 (no font size listed).

3) Windows will either prompt you for your Windows Set Up disks or tell you you have a videodriver on your system already and ask if you if you would like to use it. If it asks you for your Windows disk follow the instructions that appear on the screen. If it asks you if you want to use the current driver or install anew one, choose current.

4) restart windows as instructed by the system

   Make sure to save any vital files before making any changes to your Windows system settings. Only make these changes if you are sure your system will support them.

GLOSSARY

ASSETS:

Cash

Cash and any other valued currency that may be converted into cash such as money orders, checks, bank drafts, certificates of deposit, trade acceptances, letters of credit.

Current Assets

Unrestricted cash or other assets held for conversion, within a relatively short period, into cash or other similar assets, or useful goods or services.

Usually the period is one year or less.

The customary subdivisions of this category are: Cash, Temporary or Short-term Investments (such as Repo's, Certificates of Deposit), Accounts Receivable, Inventory, and Prepaid Expenses.

Accounts Receivable

The total sum of Accounts and Notes Receivable due from customers, resulting from sales made in the ordinary course of business.

Inventory

The total sum of Finished Goods, Raw Materials and Supplies, Work-in-Process, and Merchandise on hand.

Raw Materials are those goods purchased for use as an ingredient component part of a finished product. They range from goods in their natural state requiring further treatment or fabrication, to finished parts that may be assembled without further processing. They do not include supplies used in the manufacturing process that do not become a part of the product.

Work-in-Process or Progress is the partly finished product of a manufacturing concern. It is usually included in the inventory at the cost of the direct material and labor, plus a portion of factory overhead (or indirect expense).

Finished Goods are either manufactured product(s) or products purchased in a completed state ready for sale or other disposition to the end user-- the customer or consumer.

Other Current Assets

These are assets that have a useful life greater than one accounting period. Typically, these items are Prepaid Expenses such as Insurance, Taxes, Rent, Interest, etc.

Depreciable Assets

These items are assets having a useful life greater than one year. They are assets that diminish in value through their use. Typical items are Buildings, Machinery & Equipment, Office Furniture & Fixtures, Motor Vehicles, Computers, and Building or Leasehold Improvements.

Additionally, there is another category entitled Intangible Assets, which are amortized over their useful, tax or contract lives. Such items include Goodwill, Software Development Costs, and Patents & Trademarks. For the purposes of this presentation, the asset values should be included with all other depreciable items. The amortization should be included with depreciation.

Accumulated Depreciation (also known as Reserve for Depreciation)

These accounts represent the total (Accumulation) depreciation taken on assets since their date of acquisition, as of a given Balance Sheet date.

For each category of Depreciable Assets, their is a defined useful life.

As a general rule the following are the useful lives for each category listed above:

Buildings	40 year life.
Machinery & Equipment	10 year life.
Office Furniture & Fixtures	10 year life.
Motor Vehicles:	
Cars	3-5 year life.
Trucks	5-7 year life.
Computers	5 year life.
Building Improvements	28 year life.
Leasehold Improvements	Life of the lease.
Intangible Assets	
Goodwill	40 year life.
Patents	17 year life.

Long-term Assets

These are items having a useful life of greater than one year. Typical items in this category are Deposits, Deferred Items (such as Taxes, Compensation).

LIABILITIES:

Current Liabilities

These items represent short-term indebtedness, regardless of their source, including any liability accrued and deferred, and unearned revenue that is to be paid out of current assets or is to be transferred to income within a relatively short period of time, usually one year or less.

Accounts Payable

Any amount owing to a creditor, generally on open account, as a result of delivered goods or completed services, arising out of everyday transactions.

For the purposes of this Business Plan, we have separated this category in two subsections. One for inventory items and the second for non-inventory items.

Collectively they are known as Accounts Payable.

Short-term Debt

Short term debt, typically Bank borrowings, is the amount of debt payments due within one year. It also includes the current portion of Long-term Debt (twelve months of payments).

Debt listed here may be from any source, Bank borrowings under a line of credit, term borrowings (e.g.: 90 day notes or longer), credit card debt(s), or any other secured type of borrowing.

Accrued Expenses

This is another type of Balance Sheet liability. This category represents the recording (estimating or accruing) of expenses that are known to occur (e.g.: Professional Fees, Commissions, Royalties, Operating Expenses) but which have not been invoiced from vendors as of the Balance Sheet date.

These items should be shown under the category of Accounts Payable-Non Inventory.

Income Taxes Due

These are all of the amounts due by the business to all taxing authorities, both Federal, State and Local. Typically, taxes are remitted to these authorities on a quarterly basis.

EQUITY:

Equity is the interest of an owner(s) in the business. For the purposes of this Business Plan package, it is considered to be the Net Worth of the organization.

Stock and Paid-in Capital

Stock (Capital) represents the value of Common (and/or Preferred) Shares issued by the Corporation as evidenced by Stock Certificates. It represents the total amount of monies invested in the company.

Paid-in capital is any additional capital contributions by stockholders credited to accounts other than capital stock.

Retained Earnings

This category represents the accumulated profits and/or losses, after income taxes, of the business, since the date of inception.

It is also referred to as the Net Worth or Equity of the business.

REVENUES:

Sales

Sales are a business transaction involving the delivery of a commodity, an item of merchandise, or property, a right or service in exchange for cash, a promise to pay, or monetary equivalent, or for any combination of these items.

Sales in this Business Plan package are designed to be "Net Sales," that is Gross Invoice amounts less Returns and Allowances, Discounts, Price Adjustments, or any other direct reduction of the amount invoiced.

COST OF SALES:

Cost of Sales

The total value of inventory items sold, plus related Freight-in charges. See Inventory description above.

For service businesses, Cost of Sales represents Direct Labor dollars expended to perform the given service.

OPERATING EXPENSES:

Commissions

The remuneration of an employee or agent relating to services performed in connection with sales, purchases, collections, or other types of business transactions, and usually based upon a percentage of the amounts involved.

Marketing Expenses

This represents samples, promotional items, flyers, give-aways and any other item(s) used to attract customers and ultimately lead to sales. Trade shows, conferences, and convention expenses are included.

Payroll

The gross amounts paid to employees. This category includes all Selling, General & Administrative, Operations and Overhead personnel.

Direct Labor employees should be charged to the Cost of Sales area expenses.

Payroll Taxes and Benefits

Payroll Taxes include the employers match of FICA and Medicare withholdings, FUTA, State and Local Disability Unemployment Insurance charges.

Benefits include any amounts paid by the employer, net of employee withholdings, for Health Insurance, Life Insurance, Disability Insurance, 401(k) costs, SEP's, Pension and/or Profit Sharing plans and any other type of employee benefit expenses borne by the company.

Rent

The fee paid to a third party for the use of a facility (Building or Office Rent), equipment (for any type of Production, Distribution, or General Office use).

Utilities, Phone, Postage

Utilities include all charges for Electricity, Gas, and Water.

Phone charges include all costs of Telephone (both local and long distance), Fax and Internet Service Providers.

Postage costs include all mailing costs including, meter charges, postage, post cards, business mail charges, courier, Fedex, and other overnight costs.

Insurance

Insurance costs include all business related coverages, excluding Health Insurance listed above under Payroll Taxes & Benefits. Typical coverages are Workers Compensation, Property, Comprehensive General Liability, Motor Vehicle, Inland Marine, Employment, Directors & Officers Insurance, and all other corporate coverages.

Freight

Freight costs include all shipping charges incurred in the shipping of products to customers. Typical charges include Roadway, RPS, and all other common carriers, as well as any direct charges incurred with company owned vehicles.

Auto, Travel & Entertainment

Automobile charges include direct costs of ownership of vehicles, exclusive of Automobile Insurance. Gasoline, Repairs & Maintenance, Tires, etc. are charged to this account classifications.

Travel includes charges related to business, including Air Fares, Car Rentals, and reimbursements of employees personal use of their vehicles.

Entertainment includes business related meals and customer/client entertainment expenses.

Legal and Accounting

Professional fees for outside accountants, lawyers, and any other professional organizations.

Other Outside Services

Typically used for Consulting Fees, Service and Maintenance Contracts.

Misc. Taxes and Fees

Charges include, Real Estate Taxes, Personal Property Taxes, Licenses and Fees, and other Miscellaneous filing fees.

Depreciation

The charge representing the recovery of cost of capitalized equipment over a fixed period according to accounting guideline lives.

Other G & A Expenses

Other General & Administrative costs include, supplies, data processing expenses, temporary help, dues and subscriptions, bad debts expenses, disposal costs, and all other expenses not specified elsewhere.

Interest Expense

The charges assessed on all forms of debt (Notes Payable, Bank Borrowings, Other Loans), plus any points, origination fees, discount fees or other charges associated with borrowings.

Income Taxes

All Federal, State, and Local Taxes based on income.

Net Profit

Total Revenues less all expenses of operations and income taxes. Commonly referred as the "Bottom Line."

ADAMS

Streetwise®

Adams Streetwise software delivers real-world solutions to everyday business challenges through the use of interactive exercises, multimedia workshops, forms and templates, and video/audio interviews with savvy business people.

The most complete small business software.

▲ Covers all aspects of strategy and planning
▲ In-depth coverage of marketing, selling, and advertising
▲ Complete legal guide
▲ 30 hours of video and audio
▲ 200 multimedia workshops
▲ 100 forms and templates

Success magazine's
"The Best Business CD-ROMS"

UPC: 045079007444
ISBN: 1-55850-744-2

Save Time, Money, and Get Results!

▲ 2500 Ready-to-use Business Letters
▲ 150 Ready-to-use Forms
▲ Letters & Forms categorized for quick references
▲ Each document is completely customizable
▲ Edit as much or as little as you want

UPC: 045079201095
ISBN: 1-58062-109-0

Be your own ad agency.

▲ Write, design, and create great ads
▲ Templates for developing marketing strategies
▲ The "big idea" incubator for stimulating creativity
▲ Interactive exercises for writing professional quality copy
▲ Produce finished print ads

UPC: 045079007468
ISBN: 1-55850-746-9

The most effective way to sell in today's market.

▲ Interactive pre-call worksheets
▲ Proven ways to find the right prospect
▲ "Sales Coach" helps you handle the classic issues that trip up the sale
▲ Ready-to-use sales letter templates

UPC: 045079008335
ISBN: 1-55850-833-3

Explore hundreds of today's most exciting small businesses.

▲ Interactive questionnaire to select the most appropriate businesses
▲ In-depth information on each business includes start-up cost, earnings potential, typical pricing, best advertising bets, "inside advice," and more
▲ Two hours of video/audio interviews with business owners
▲ Includes home, part-time, and computer-based businesses

UPC: 045079007420
ISBN: 1-55850-742-6

Hire the right people the first time.

▲ For both small business owners and corporate managers
▲ 600 ready-to-select interview questions
▲ Just choose and print your questions
▲ Videos help improve interview skills
▲ 25 workshops cover all aspects of hiring

UPC: 045079007475
ISBN: 1-55850-747-7

Designed for
Microsoft **Windows®95**

All products include both native Win95 and Win 3.1 versions.

Mac OS

All products except 500 Businesses and Hiring Top Performers include MAC versions.

CD-ROM

All products include CD-ROM multimedia versions.

3.5" DISK

All products include "lite" 3.5" disk versions.

Available at software retailers nationwide.

Please look for these titles at your favorite software retail outlet.
For more information, call Adams Media Corporation at 1-800-872-5627.

Visit our exciting small business website: careercity.com

Software License Agreement

YOU SHOULD CAREFULLY READ THE FOLLOWING TERMS AND CONDITIONS BEFORE USING THIS SOFTWARE PRODUCT. INSTALLING AND USING THIS PRODUCT INDICATES YOUR ACCEPTANCE OF THESE CONDITIONS. IF YOU DO NOT AGREE WITH THESE TERMS AND CONDITIONS, DO NOT INSTALL THE SOFTWARE AND RETURN THIS PACKAGE PROMPTLY FOR A FULL REFUND.

1. Grant of License:

This software package is protected under United States copyright law and international treaty. You are hereby entitled to one copy of the enclosed software and are allowed by law to make one backup copy or to copy the contents of the disks onto a single hard disk and keep the originals as your backup or archival copy. United States copyright law prohibits you from making a copy of this software for use on any computer other than your own computer. United States copyright law also prohibits you from copying any written material included in this software package without first obtaining the permission of Adams Media Corporation.

2. Restrictions:

You, the end-user, are hereby prohibited from the following:

You may not rent or lease the Software or make copies to rent or lease for profit or for any other purpose.

You may not disassemble or reverse compile for the purposes of reverse engineering the Software.

You may not modify or adapt the Software or documentation in whole or in part, including, but not limited to, translating or creating derivative works.

3. Transfer:

You may transfer the Software to another person, provided that (a) you transfer all of the Software and documentation to the same transferee; (b) you do not retain any copies; and (c) the transferee is informed of and agrees to the terms and conditions of this Agreement

4. Termination:

This Agreement and your license to use the Software can be terminated without notice if you fail to comply with any of the provisions set forth in this Agreement. Upon termination of this Agreement, you promise to destroy all copies of the software including backup or archival copies as well as any documentation associated with the Software. All disclaimers of warranties and limitation of liability set forth in this Agreement shall survive any termination of this Agreement.

5. Limited Warranty

Adams Media Corporation warrants that the Software will perform according to the manual and other written materials accompanying the Software for a period of 30 days from the date of receipt. Adams Media Corporation does not accept responsibility for any malfunctioning computer hardware or any incompatibilities with existing or new computer hardware technology.

6. Customer Remedies

Adams Media Corporation's entire liability and your exclusive remedy shall be, at the option of Adams Media Corporation, either refund of your purchase price or repair and/or replacement of Software that does not meet this Limited Warranty. Proof of purchase shall be required. This Limited Warranty will be voided if Software failure was caused by abuse, neglect, accident or misapplication. All replacement Software will be warranted based on the remainder of the warranty or the full 30 days, whichever is shorter and will be subject to the terms of the Agreement.

7. No Other Warranties

ADAMS MEDIA CORPORATION, TO THE FULLEST EXTENT OF THE LAW, DISCLAIMS ALL OTHER WARRANTIES, OTHER THAN THE LIMITED WARRANTY IN PARAGRAPH 5, EITHER EXPRESS OR IMPLIED, ASSOCIATED WITH ITS SOFTWARE, INCLUDING BUT NOT LIMITED TO IMPLIED WARRANTIES OF MERCHANTABILITY AND FITNESS FOR A PARTICULAR PURPOSE, WITH REGARD TO THE SOFTWARE AND ITS ACCOMPANYING WRITTEN MATERIALS. THIS LIMITED WARRANTY GIVES YOU SPECIFIC LEGAL RIGHTS. DEPENDING UPON WHERE THIS SOFTWARE WAS PURCHASED, YOU MAY HAVE OTHER RIGHTS.

8. Limitations on Remedies

TO THE MAXIMUM EXTENT PERMITTED BY LAW, ADAMS MEDIA CORPORATION SHALL NOT BE HELD LIABLE FOR ANY DAMAGES WHATSOEVER, INCLUDING WITHOUT LIMITATION, ANY LOSS FROM PERSONAL INJURY, LOSS OF BUSINESS PROFITS, BUSINESS INTERRUPTION, BUSINESS INFORMATION OR ANY OTHER PECUNIARY LOSS ARISING OUT OF THE USE OF THIS SOFTWARE.

This applies even if Adams Media Corporation has been advised of the possibility of such damages. Adams Media Corporation's entire liability under any provision of this agreement shall be limited to the amount actually paid by you for the Software. Because some states may not allow for this type of limitation of liability, the above limitation may not apply to you.

THE WARRANTY AND REMEDIES SET FORTH ABOVE ARE EXCLUSIVE AND IN LIEU OF ALL OTHERS, ORAL OR WRITTEN, EXPRESS OR IMPLIED. No Adams Media Corporation dealer, distributor, agent, or employee is authorized to make any modification or addition to the warranty.

General

This Agreement shall be governed by the laws of the United States of America and the Commonwealth of Massachusetts.

You must fill out and return the Adams New Media registration card to be eligible for customer support and service. If you have any questions concerning this Agreement, contact Adams New Media at 617-767-8100. Or write to us at:

Adams Media Corporation
260 Center Street
Holbrook, MA 02343